# VCE Units 3 & 4
# BUSINESS MANAGEMENT

**AMANDA RITTER | KIRSTEN FURNESS**

A+

2023-2027 STUDY DESIGN • 2023-2027 STUDY DESIGN •

+ 12 topic tests
+ 2 complete practice exams
+ detailed, annotated solutions

# PRACTICE
# EXAMS

A+ VCE Business Management Practice Exams
Amanda Ritter
Kirsten Furness
ISBN 9780170465120

Publisher: Caroline Williams
Project editor: Tanya Smith
Editor: Leanne Peters
Series text design: Nikita Bansal
Series cover design: Nikita Bansal
Series designer: Cengage Creative Studio
Artwork: MPS Limited
Production controller: Karen Young
Typeset by: Nikki M Group Pty Ltd

Any URLs contained in this publication were checked for currency during the production process. Note, however, that the publisher cannot vouch for the ongoing currency of URLs.

Acknowledgements

Selected VCE examination questions and extracts from the VCE Study Designs are copyright Victorian Curriculum and Assessment Authority (VCAA), reproduced by permission. VCE ® is a registered trademark of the VCAA. The VCAA does not endorse this product and makes no warranties regarding the correctness or accuracy of this study resource. To the extent permitted by law, the VCAA excludes all liability for any loss or damage suffered or incurred as a result of accessing, using or relying on the content. Current VCE Study Designs, past VCE exams and related content can be accessed directly at www.vcaa.vic.edu.au.

For product information and technology assistance,
in Australia call **1300 790 853;**
in New Zealand call **0800 449 725**

For permission to use material from this text or product, please email **aust.permissions@cengage.com**

ISBN 978 0 17 046512 0

**Cengage Learning Australia**
Level 7, 80 Dorcas Street
South Melbourne, Victoria Australia 3205

**Cengage Learning New Zealand**
Unit 4B Rosedale Office Park
331 Rosedale Road, Albany, North Shore 0632, NZ

For learning solutions, visit **cengage.com.au**

Printed in China by 1010 Printing International Limited.
1 2 3 4 5 6 7 26 25 24 23 22

# CONTENTS

## UNIT 3

### MANAGING A BUSINESS

#### Area of Study 1

#### Area of Study 2

#### Area of Study 3

#### Areas of Study 1–3

## UNIT 4

### TRANSFORMING A BUSINESS

#### Area of Study 1

#### Area of Study 2

#### Areas of Study 1–2

## PRACTICE EXAMS

9780170465120

# HOW TO USE THIS BOOK

The *A+ Business Management* resources are designed to be used year-round to prepare you for your VCE Business Management exam. *A+ Business Management Practice Exams* includes 12 topic tests and two practice exams, plus detailed solutions for all questions in this resource. This section gives you a brief overview of the features included in this resource.

## Topic tests

Each topic test is on one key knowledge area of the Study Design and for each unit, there is a unit test (Test 7 and Test 12). The tests follow the same sequence as the Study Design, starting with the first key knowledge area of Unit 3, 'Business foundations', and ending with the final key knowledge area of Unit 4, 'Implementing change'. The topic tests include a range of structured and case study questions, including a selection of past VCAA exam questions. Hints have been included to provide guidance on exam strategy, as well as on how best to approach different types of questions and avoid common mistakes.

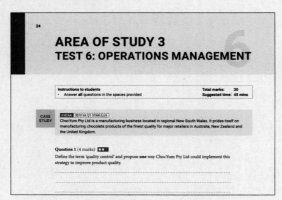 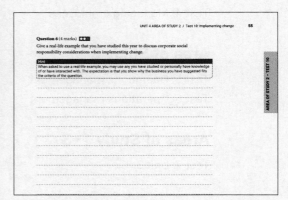

## Practice exam section

Both practice exams cover all of Units 3 and 4 of the VCE Business Management Study Design. The practice exams have perforated pages so that you can remove them from the book and practise under exam-style conditions.

## Solutions

Solutions to the test and exam questions are supplied at the back of the book. They have been written to model high-scoring responses and include some student response examples from previous VCAA examiners' reports.

### Explanations

The solutions section for the topic tests includes explanations to give students additional insights, support to understand what a high-scoring response looks like, and highlights potential mistakes and common misconceptions.

### Mark breakdown

Each solution is accompanied by a detailed mark breakdown to assist students in understanding how responses are marked and to inform their exam preparation.

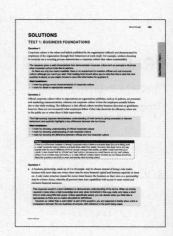

# Icons

You will notice the following icons in the topic tests.

This icon appears next to official past VCAA exam questions.

This icon signifies the difficulty of each question in the topic tests. One of these icons appears next to all questions to indicate whether the question is easy, medium or hard.

# About *A+ Business Management Study Notes*

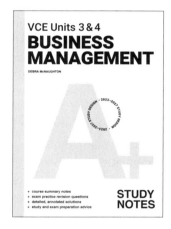 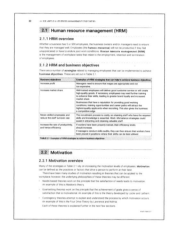

*A+ Business Management Practice Exams* can be used independently or alongside the accompanying resource, *A+ Business Management Study Notes*. *A+ Business Management Study Notes* includes topic summaries of all key knowledge in the VCE Business Management Study Design 2023–2027 that you will be assessed on during your exam. This book also includes revision summaries and practice exam questions with solutions that have been written to model high-scoring responses, as well as detailed explanations.

# A+ DIGITAL FLASHCARDS

Revise key terms and concepts online with the A+ Flashcards. Each topic glossary in the *A+ Business Management Study Notes* has a corresponding deck of digital flashcards you can use to test your understanding and recall. Just scan the QR code or type the URL into your browser to access them. Note: You will need to create a free NelsonNet account.

https://get.ga/aplus-vcebusmgmt-u34

9780170465120

# ABOUT THE AUTHORS

## Amanda Ritter MAEd (global), BA, DipEd (Secondary), GCUT, pursuing GCER

Amanda Ritter has extensive experience in secondary Commerce education as a teacher, mentor, teacher leader, article and awarded textbook writer, online presenter for students, professional development presenter both in Victoria and interstate, and statewide professional association journal editor. As a lecturer in initial teacher education, Amanda has coordinated the Commerce suite of subjects for the Melbourne Graduate School of Education (MGSE) Secondary Master of Teaching course and supervised teacher candidates on placement. Her current roles include Regional Coordinator within the Quality Teaching Branch at the Department of Education and Training, where she assists regional and low Index of Community Socio-Educational Advantage (ICSEA) schools to attract high-performing pre-service graduate teachers. She values access to education for all, vocational training, encouraging more girls to study business and economics, facilitating student voice, active learning and active citizenship, as well as effective use of information and communication technologies (ICT) in the classroom. Amanda strives to make learning personalised, meaningful and relevant for students, so they can recognise and value their own individual strengths, take positive action, be empowered to control their own learning journey and ultimately be their best selves through education. This book provides motivated students with a tool to progress their own learning, as they prepare for high-stakes assessments.

## Kirsten Furness MEd (Mgt), BBusCom, BCom, DipEd (Secondary), GCED, GCER

Kirsten Furness is an experienced teacher of Business Management and Accounting and an educational leader in pedagogy, curriculum and assessment. Kirsten has worked as a curriculum writer for the Victorian Curriculum and Assessment Authority. She has been a regular contributor to the Victorian Commercial Teachers Association's *Compak* journal and has delivered professional learning at its annual conference, *Comview*. Kirsten was the recipient of the 2019 Monash University Dean's Award for Academic Excellence Graduate Certificate of Education for her thesis *Disciplinary literacy perspectives in VCE Business Management*.

# UNIT 3
# MANAGING A BUSINESS

# AREA OF STUDY 1
## TEST 1: BUSINESS FOUNDATIONS

| Instructions to students | Total marks: 30 |
| --- | --- |
| • Answer **all** questions in the spaces provided | Suggested time: 45 mins |

**Question 1** (2 marks)

Define the term 'corporate culture'.

_____

_____

_____

_____

_____

**Question 2** (3 marks)

Distinguish between official and real corporate culture.

_____

_____

_____

_____

_____

_____

_____

_____

_____

**Question 3** (4 marks)

a  ©VCAA 2017 SA Q1b  ○●● Outline **one** reason why a business may choose to operate as a partnership rather than as a sole trader.                    2 marks

_____

_____

_____

_____

_____

b  ○●● Describe **one** disadvantage of structuring a business as a partnership.                    2 marks

_____

_____

_____

_____

**Question 4** (10 marks)

a  ●●○ Identify **one** type of business and give a real-life example.                    2 marks

> **Hint**
> There are no wrong answers when giving a real-life example. In fact, you may name a business the assessor doesn't even know. The important thing is to clearly explain a business type and how your selected business fits that type.

_____

_____

_____

_____

_____

**b** ⬤⬤⬤ For the business type identified in question 4a, propose and justify an appropriate business objective.    3 marks

> **Hint**
> The task word 'propose' asks for your opinion. Draw on key knowledge to suggest an appropriate response, choosing an objective that you feel confident writing about.

_____

_____

_____

_____

_____

_____

_____

_____

_____

**c** ⬤⬤⬤ For the same business type named in question 4a, identify **two** stakeholders.    2 marks

_____

_____

_____

_____

**d** ⬤⬤⬤ Explain a potential conflict between the stakeholders identified in question 4c.    3 marks

_____

_____

_____

_____

_____

_____

_____

_____

_____

**Question 5** (2 marks) ⬤⚪⚪

Define the term 'interpersonal skills'.

_____

_____

_____

_____

_____

**Question 6** (3 marks) ⬤⬤⚪

Explain a likely impact on employees if a manager does not effectively apply the management skill of 'communication'.

_____

_____

_____

_____

_____

_____

_____

_____

_____

**Question 7** (3 marks) ⬤⬤⬤

State and justify a management style that is appropriate to use with experienced employees.

_____

_____

_____

_____

_____

_____

_____

_____

**Question 8** (3 marks) ⬤⬤⬤

Discuss how an autocratic manager may use the management skill of delegation.

_____

_____

_____

_____

_____

_____

_____

_____

# AREA OF STUDY 1
## TEST 2: BUSINESS FOUNDATIONS

| Instructions to students | Total marks: | 30 |
|---|---|---|
| • Answer **all** questions in the spaces provided | Suggested time: | 45 mins |

## Question 1 (3 marks) ⬤⬤▫

With reference to a contemporary case study, explain the purpose of a government business enterprise.

_____

_____

_____

_____

_____

_____

_____

_____

_____

## Question 2 (15 marks)

Beautiful Blooms is a florist that currently operates as a sole trader. Due to a significant increase in profit, a manager has been appointed and has recommended the owner change the structure of the business to a private limited company.

**a** ©VCAA 2021 SA Q1a ⬤▫▫ With reference to this business, define the term 'stakeholder'.     2 marks

> **Hint**
> When defining a term, aim to include two key parts of the definition in your answer.

_____

_____

_____

_____

_____

_____

**b** ●○■ Compare the characteristics of a social enterprise and a private limited company.    4 marks

_____

_____

_____

_____

_____

_____

_____

_____

_____

_____

**c** ○■■ Other than 'to make a profit', describe **one** business objective for Beautiful Blooms.    2 marks

_____

_____

_____

_____

_____

_____

**d** ●●■ Decision-making is a management skill. Explain how the owner of Beautiful Blooms may use this skill to decide whether to change the structure of the business to a private limited company.    3 marks

_____

_____

_____

_____

_____

_____

_____

e  ▦▦▦  Analyse how the interests of the manager and suppliers of Beautiful Blooms may be in conflict.                                                                          4 marks

> **Hint**
> The task word 'analyse' requires you to consider cause and effect; what are the interests of each stakeholder and, consequently, how might these interests be in conflict?

_____

_____

_____

_____

_____

_____

_____

_____

_____

_____

**Question 3** (12 marks)

Arrow Sports operates seven stores in Victoria. With an increased demand for online shopping, Gary, the owner of Arrow Sports, has decided to close three stores within 12 months in order for Arrow Sports to have the resources to improve the website, increase online sales and improve effectiveness. Thirty per cent of existing employees will continue to be employed by Arrow Sports and 70% will be made redundant. Gary intends to use a consultative style of management during this period of change.

a  ▦▦▦  Explain how the closure of three stores may help Arrow Sports to achieve the business objective of improving effectiveness.                                           3 marks

_____

_____

_____

_____

**b**  ◖◗◗◗  Evaluate the appropriateness of Gary using the consultative management style during the period of change.                                                                5 marks

_____

_____

_____

_____

_____

_____

_____

_____

_____

_____

_____

_____

_____

_____

_____

_____

**c**  ◖◗◗  Outline **two** management skills Gary will need to use during the store closures.                                                                4 marks

_____

_____

_____

_____

_____

_____

_____

_____

_____

_____

_____

_____

# AREA OF STUDY 2
## TEST 3: MANAGING EMPLOYEES

| Instructions to students | Total marks: | 30 |
|---|---|---|
| • Answer **all** questions in the spaces provided | Suggested time: | 45 mins |

**Question 1** (2 marks)

Define the term 'sanction strategy'.

_____

_____

_____

_____

_____

**Question 2** (1 mark)

Identify a motivation strategy that could have a positive long-term impact on employee motivation.

_____

_____

_____

**Question 3** (2 marks)

Describe the relationship between human resource management and business objectives.

_____

_____

_____

_____

_____

_____

**Question 4** (10 marks)

a    Outline the key principles of Lawrence and Nohria's Four Drive Theory of Motivation.  4 marks

_____

_____

_____

_____

_____

_____

_____

_____

_____

_____

_____

b    Demonstrate one way a manager might apply Lawrence and Nohria's theory to motivate workers.      2 marks

_____

_____

_____

_____

_____

c    Compare Lawrence and Nohria's motivation theory to Locke and Latham's Goal Setting motivation theory.      4 marks

_____

_____

_____

_____

_____

_____

_____

_____

**Question 5** (5 marks)

a  `◖◖◗` Distinguish between on-the-job and off-the-job training.     3 marks

_____

_____

_____

_____

_____

_____

_____

_____

b  `◖◖◗` Training can be expensive in many ways. Discuss one cost to the business of
investing in on-the-job training.     2 marks

_____

_____

_____

_____

_____

**Question 6** (10 marks)

Anthony is a middle manager at the large electronics producer and retailer Corporate
Electrical, with a department sales turnover in the millions. He has an experienced team
of lower manager supervisors and he trusts them to deal with their staff professionally to
meet the set business objectives handed down from senior managers. Anthony has effective
interpersonal skills, knows his staff well and has built productive working relationships with
most employees. Anthony uses a laissez-faire style, as he prefers to set and communicate
targets and then leave his experienced staff to get on with their jobs. As a manager, Anthony
delegates effectively and is respected as a well-organised planner. Despite his competent
management, and recently combining an employee training seminar and golf day to develop
better teamwork, worker surveys report a loss in motivation. Staff turnover is on the rise
as some supervisors look elsewhere for higher remuneration, mentoring to improve career
prospects or more challenges to improve job satisfaction.

a  `◖◗◗` Identify the type of training mentioned in the case study.     1 mark

_____

_____

b ⬤◯◻ State **two** advantages of the type of training identified in question 6a.    2 marks

> **Hint**
> If an incorrect type of training is identified in question 6a, the phrasing of question 6b still allows for a full two marks to be awarded for advantages related to the previously stated type of training.

c ◼◼◼ Other than investment in training, propose and justify a motivation strategy to improve employee motivation in the short term at Corporate Electrical.    3 marks

d ©VCAA  2018 SA Q1c (MODIFIED) ⬤⬤◻ Maslow's Hierarchy of Needs has been suggested to Anthony as an appropriate motivational theory for improving employee performance. Briefly describe this theory of motivation and explain how it could be applied at Corporate Electrical to reduce the level of staff turnover.    4 marks

> **Hint**
> Common in an exam question is the need to 'apply a theory to a business simulation or case study'. Unless it is a 10-mark question, often there are not enough marks allocated for all elements of a theory or concept to be applied. However, you still need to have a detailed working knowledge of each of the theories and how they can be used by managers in practice to improve worker motivation, so you can choose the best parts to include in your response. Remember to clearly link back to whatever business scenario is provided to demonstrate your understanding of how to apply theory in practical business situations.

# AREA OF STUDY 2
# TEST 4: MANAGING EMPLOYEES

| Instructions to students | | |
|---|---|---|
| • Answer **all** questions in the spaces provided | Total marks: | 30 |
| | Suggested time: | 45 mins |

**Question 1** (2 marks) ⬤⬤⬤

Define the term 'performance management'.

_____

_____

_____

_____

_____

**Question 2** (4 marks) ⬤⬤⬤

Explain how management by objectives can be used as a strategy to achieve both business and employee objectives.

> **Hint**
>
> It is important to read the question as two parts: 1. How can management by objectives be used to achieve business objectives? and 2. How can management by objectives be used to achieve employee objectives? Using paragraphs to structure your response will help to highlight that you have attended to both parts of the question.

_____

_____

_____

_____

_____

_____

_____

_____

_____

**Question 3** (3 marks) ⬤⬤⬤

Propose and justify **one** performance management strategy to improve the efficiency of a business.

_____

_____

_____

_____

_____

_____

_____

_____

**Question 4** (17 marks)

V-Steel is a large steel manufacturer, located in regional Victoria. V-Steel employs 230 people, with the majority working in permanent full-time or part-time roles. V-Steel uses an agreement to determine pay and conditions, and the current agreement is due to expire at the end of 2029.

**a**    ⬤◻◻    Describe the roles of employees and the Fair Work Commission in a workplace such as V-Steel.                                                                4 marks

> **Hint**
> Careful reading of this question and stimulus material is necessary to identify what you need to include in your response.

_____

_____

_____

_____

_____

_____

_____

_____

_____

_____

**b** ◼◻◻ Discuss the use of an agreement to determine wages and conditions of work.     4 marks

_____

_____

_____

_____

_____

_____

_____

_____

_____

_____

**c** ◼◼◻ Compare awards and agreements as methods of determining wages and conditions of work.     4 marks

> **Hint**
> Watch out! This is NOT the same question as the one before. Although there may be some similar points made, the task word is asking for a different approach.

_____

_____

_____

_____

_____

_____

_____

_____

_____

_____

_____

**d** ☐☐☐ Miya works part-time and is currently involved in a dispute with management about the safety practices at V-Steel.

Evaluate an appropriate dispute resolution process that could be used to resolve the dispute between Miya and the management of V-Steel.

5 marks

_____

_____

_____

_____

_____

_____

_____

_____

_____

_____

_____

_____

**Question 5** (4 marks) ☐☐☐

Distinguish between dismissal and redundancy.

Within your response, include reference to the entitlement considerations and transition considerations associated with each termination method.

_____

_____

_____

_____

_____

_____

_____

_____

_____

_____

_____

# AREA OF STUDY 3
## TEST 5: OPERATIONS MANAGEMENT

**Instructions to students**
· Answer **all** questions in the spaces provided

**Total marks:** 30
**Suggested time:** 45 mins

©VCAA 2020 SA Q5 STIMULUS

Chef@Home aims to transform the way people prepare meals in their homes. The business delivers all the ingredients required to cook a meal, in a chilled box, to customers' homes.

CASE STUDY

Chef@Home is committed to minimising its carbon footprint, especially through the elimination of waste. All boxes, bags and containers used by the business are recyclable. Ingredients are prepared and packaged using automated production lines. Chef@Home has a policy of sourcing all inputs from local suppliers. Forecasting is a key component of its business operations.

At times, Chef@Home's local suppliers have been unable to source and deliver orders placed by the business. Consequently, Chef@Home is considering whether to source some ingredients from overseas suppliers.

**Question 1** (3 marks)

Outline the relationship between operations management and **one** business objective of Chef@Home.

> **Hint**
> To successfully respond to this question, you need to infer (derive through reasoning or 'read between the lines') certain details about Chef@Home as a business in order to make logical links between operations management and business objectives.

**Question 2** (5 marks) ⬤⬤⬜

Identify the **three** key elements of the operations system. Apply **two** of these elements to Chef@Home.

> **Hint**
> One mark is allocated to the identification of the three elements of the operations system – so even if you give two correct elements, you cannot be awarded the mark without all three.

_____

_____

_____

_____

_____

_____

_____

_____

_____

_____

_____

_____

_____

_____

**Question 3** (4 marks)  ©VCAA  2020 SA Q5b  ⬤⬤⬤

Analyse how forecasting might be used by Chef@Home to improve the efficiency and effectiveness of its operations.

> **Hint**
> Because they are mentioned separately in the question, you need to treat efficiency and effectiveness as two separate concepts in your response, and include reference to both.

_____

_____

_____

_____

_____

_____

_____

_____

_____

_____

**Question 4** (3 marks)  ⬤⬤◐

Examine the use of 'recycle' as a strategy to minimise waste at Chef@Home.

> **Hint**
> 'Examine' involves considering the concept in a way that considers possibilities or interrelationships.

_____

_____

_____

_____

_____

_____

_____

**Question 5** (4 marks)  ◐◼◼

Describe how corporate social responsibility considerations may influence decisions made by the management of Chef@Home in relation to the operations system.

_____

_____

_____

_____

_____

_____

_____

_____

_____

_____

**Question 6** (5 marks) ⬤⬤⬤

Evaluate the use of an automated production line at Chef@Home as a strategy to improve the efficiency of operations.

_____

_____

_____

_____

_____

_____

_____

_____

_____

_____

_____

_____

_____

_____

**Question 7** (6 marks)  ©VCAA  2020 SA Q5c  ●●

The managers of Chef@Home are reviewing the business's supply chain management in an effort to improve business competitiveness.

Discuss the considerations the managers should take into account when deciding whether to source some ingredients from overseas suppliers.

> **Hint**
> A description or explanation of considerations is not sufficient to gain full marks. The task word 'discuss' requires you to weigh up the advantages and disadvantages of the considerations presented in your response. However, unlike with the task word 'evaluate', 'discuss' does not require you to provide a conclusion based on your reasons.

# AREA OF STUDY 3
# TEST 6: OPERATIONS MANAGEMENT

6

| Instructions to students | |
|---|---|
| • Answer **all** questions in the spaces provided | **Total marks:** 30 <br> **Suggested time:** 45 mins |

**CASE STUDY**

©VCAA 2019 SA Q1 STIMULUS
ChocYum Pty Ltd is a manufacturing business located in regional New South Wales. It prides itself on manufacturing chocolate products of the finest quality for major retailers in Australia, New Zealand and the United Kingdom.

## Question 1 (4 marks) ●●□

Define the term 'quality control' and propose **one** way ChocYum Pty Ltd could implement this strategy to improve product quality.

_____

_____

_____

_____

_____

_____

_____

_____

_____

_____

**Question 2** (4 marks)   ©VCAA   2019 SA Q1b   ●●

Compare the characteristics of operations management within a manufacturing business (such as ChocYum Pty Ltd) with those of a service business.

> **Hint**
>
> The task word 'compare' requires that both similarities and differences be discussed. Often it does not matter whether there is an even number discussed, just as long as there is at least one of each.

_____

_____

_____

_____

_____

_____

_____

_____

_____

_____

_____

**Question 3** (3 marks)   ●○○○

Other than an automated production line, identify and describe **one** technological development strategy that could be implemented at ChocYum Pty Ltd.

_____

_____

_____

_____

_____

_____

_____

**Question 4** (2 marks) 🔲🔲⬛

Other than forecasting, propose **one** strategy to improve the efficiency or effectiveness of materials management at ChocYum.

> **Hint**
> Read this question again carefully: is it 'and' or 'or'?

_____

_____

_____

_____

_____

**Question 5** (3 marks) ⬛⬛⬛

Justify how ChocYum Pty Ltd could improve efficiency through the waste minimisation strategy of 'reuse'.

_____

_____

_____

_____

_____

_____

_____

**Question 6** (6 marks)  ©VCAA  2019 SA Q1c  ●●

Explain how ChocYum Pty Ltd could implement the principles of lean management to improve the efficiency or effectiveness of its operations system.

_____

_____

_____

_____

_____

_____

_____

_____

_____

_____

_____

_____

_____

_____

**Question 7** (4 marks) ⬤⬤⬤

The owner of ChocYum Pty Ltd is considering opening a manufacturing facility in the United Kingdom.

Evaluate the global consideration of overseas manufacture for ChocYum Pty Ltd.

> **Hint**
> The task word 'evaluate' requires strengths, weaknesses and a conclusion based on what has already been mentioned. The trick is to check the marks to see how many strengths and weaknesses are required for full marks. If you do more than expected, only your first point mentioned will be marked, so you may be wasting precious test time and line space without gaining any extra marks.

**Question 8** (4 marks) ⬤⬤⬤

ChocYum Pty Ltd has committed to having a zero-carbon footprint by 2030.

Analyse **one** corporate social responsibility consideration for the operations system at ChocYum Pty Ltd in relation to environmental sustainability.

> **Hint**
>
> The task word 'analyse' requires you to break down something into component parts and show how the parts make up the whole. So, in the above case, this involves looking at specific areas of operations that could be focused on sustainability. It is always good to return to the question by the end of your response and link everything back to how the business may or may not benefit.

# AREAS OF STUDY 1–3
## TEST 7: UNIT 3

| Instructions to students | Total marks: 60 |
| --- | --- |
| • Answer **all** questions in the spaces provided | Suggested time: 90 mins |

**Question 1** (6 marks) ⬤⬤⬤

Define the following terms.

> **Hint**
> Exam definitions are awarded two marks, so some detail is needed. It can help to break your answer into two sentences, so you remember to make two clear points or give examples that demonstrate your understanding.

**a** Business objectives

2 marks

_____

_____

_____

_____

_____

_____

**b** Resignation

2 marks

_____

_____

_____

_____

_____

_____

**c**  Quality assurance                                                      2 marks

_____

_____

_____

_____

_____

_____

# Area of Study 1

DanceNow is an Australian publicly listed global dance instruction business with 22 branches in major cities. As the Chief Executive Officer (CEO), Hester has some serious issues with a few senior managers. In general, there seems to be no issue with telling them what needs to be done, as long as she is clear about the reasons decisions have been made and the potential impact on staff. Her managers are generally very satisfied with the information they receive and feel Hester is an approachable and informative leader who always lets them know what is happening and why. Her newly appointed workforce is stable and content; however, Hester has found that some managers have proven not capable of the tasks she has set. This has resulted in issues only being realised after becoming serious, such as city site enrolments being allowed to fall to crisis levels after a shift in the population, or global transport issues causing major delays on customer uniform orders and essential dance equipment. Some DanceNow branches may close and shareholders are not happy with this drop in the rate of productivity growth.

| CASE STUDY |

**Question 2** (18 marks)

**a**  ⬤◯◯  With reference to DanceNow, state and describe the type of business.          3 marks

> **Hint**
> To demonstrate clear understanding, it is best to use evidence from the case study in your answer, rather than just making a conclusion.

_____

_____

_____

_____

_____

_____

_____

_____

**b** 🔳 Distinguish between stakeholders and shareholders.    3 marks

_____

_____

_____

_____

_____

_____

_____

_____

_____

**c** 🔳 Illustrate **one** element of the real corporate culture at DanceNow.    2 marks

_____

_____

_____

_____

_____

_____

**d** 🔳 Analyse the extent to which Hester's current management style is appropriate.    4 marks

_____

_____

_____

_____

_____

_____

_____

_____

_____

_____

_____

e   Use evidence from the case study to identify **one** management skill Hester demonstrates.     2 marks

_____

_____

_____

_____

_____

f   Assess the business scenario to propose a management skill for Hester to develop to improve her effectiveness.     4 marks

_____

_____

_____

_____

_____

_____

_____

_____

_____

_____

# Area of Study 2

**STRUCTURED QUESTIONS** (18 marks)

**Question 3** (4 marks)

Outline the key principles of Maslow's Hierarchy of Needs theory of motivation.

_____

_____

_____

_____

_____

_____

_____

_____

_____

_____

_____

_____

**Question 4** (4 marks)

Demonstrate how a manager might apply Locke and Latham's Goal Setting Theory to motivate underperforming employees.

_____

_____

_____

_____

_____

_____

_____

_____

_____

_____

_____

**Question 5** (3 marks) 

Other than management by objectives, suggest and describe **one** performance management strategy to achieve both business and employee objectives.

_____

_____

_____

_____

_____

_____

_____

_____

**Question 6** (4 marks) 

As participants in the workplace, employer associations and unions often have conflicting interests. Discuss the role of unions in the workplace.

_____

_____

_____

_____

_____

_____

_____

_____

_____

_____

**Question 7** (3 marks) ●●●

Evaluate 'retirement' as a method of terminating a workplace arrangement for the employer.

_____

_____

_____

_____

_____

_____

_____

_____

_____

_____

# Area of Study 3

## STRUCTURED QUESTIONS AND SHORT STIMULUS (18 marks)

**Question 8** (2 marks) ●○○

Outline **one** technological development strategy to improve the efficiency of operations management.

_____

_____

_____

_____

_____

_____

**Question 9** (3 marks) ●●○

Explain the relationship between operations management and business objectives.

_____

_____

_____

_____

_____

_____

_____

_____

**Question 10** (3 marks) ●●●

Propose and justify how a manager might use the strategy of 'Total Quality Management' to improve the effectiveness of an operations system.

_____

_____

_____

_____

_____

_____

_____

_____

**Question 11** (4 marks) ●●○

Examine the waste minimisation strategy of 'reduce' as a method to improve the efficiency and effectiveness of operations.

_____

_____

_____

_____

_____

_____

_____

_____

_____

_____

**Question 12** (6 marks) ⬤⬤⬜

'Businesses need to get with the times and focus more on corporate social responsibility considerations in their operations, otherwise customers will not only choose competitors, they will also use social media to influence others who haven't even interacted with the business to that point, and now never will.'

This quote highlights the growing importance of corporate social responsibility for businesses. Use a real-life business example that you have studied to explain **one** corporate social responsibility consideration for an operations system and suggest **one** stakeholder of the business that may have been impacted by this strategy.

> **Hint**
> Remember that whenever you are asked to suggest something you must show how yours is a suitable suggestion.

_____

_____

_____

_____

_____

_____

_____

_____

_____

_____

_____

_____

_____

_____

_____

_____

# UNIT 4
# TRANSFORMING A BUSINESS

# AREA OF STUDY 1
## TEST 8: REVIEWING PERFORMANCE – THE NEED FOR CHANGE

| Instructions to students | Total marks: | 30 |
|---|---|---|
| • Answer **all** questions in the spaces provided | Suggested time: | 45 mins |

**Question 1** (2 marks) ⬤◯◯

Define the term 'business change'.

_____

_____

_____

_____

_____

_____

**Question 2** (4 marks) ⬤⬤◯

Compare proactive and reactive approaches to change.

_____

_____

_____

_____

_____

_____

_____

_____

_____

_____

_____

**Question 3** (5 marks) ⬤⬤⬤

Evaluate how a business can use the lower-cost approach to operate successfully in a highly competitive market.

**Question 4** (19 marks)  ©VCAA  2018 SA Q3 STIMULUS

The manager of Wilkinson's Window Tinting was disappointed with the performance of the business after one year of trading. As a result, she decided to purchase new machinery and automate the tinting process. At the end of the second year of trading, the manager examined a range of key performance indicators in order to assess the extent to which this change had been successful.

| Key performance indicator | Year 1 | Year 2 |
| --- | --- | --- |
| Net profit figure | $47 000 | $23 000 |
| Rate of productivity growth | 2% | 8% |
| Number of customer complaints | 112 | 28 |
| Rate of staff absenteeism | Average of four days per year per staff member | Average of 12 days per year per staff member |

**a**  ◖●◗  Using the information provided, describe how 'rate of productivity growth' can be used to analyse the performance of Wilkinson's Window Tinting.                          3 marks

_____

_____

_____

_____

_____

_____

_____

_____

**b**  ©VCAA  2018 SA Q3b  ●●●  With reference to the data at the start of the question, analyse the extent to which the purchase of the new machinery has assisted Wilkinson's Window Tinting in improving the performance of the business.    6 marks

> **Hint**
> While it can be tempting to refer to all of the key performance indicators (KPIs) in order to be thorough, this can lead to the response being too broad to effectively provide a comprehensive and detailed analysis. Focusing on two or three KPIs allows you to draw together a more sophisticated analysis about the link between the investment in new machinery and data trends.

**c**  ●●  Explain how the manager of Wilkinson's Window Tinting has acted as a driving force for change in the business.    3 marks

> **Hint**
> You do not need to provide definitions in your response to this question; however, it is important to demonstrate your understanding of the terms 'manager' and 'driving force' when you detail how the manager has acted as a driving force for change.

d　◖●◗　With reference to the data at the start of the question, outline how employees may be acting as a restraining force for change at Wilkinson's Window Tinting.　　　3 marks

_____

_____

_____

_____

_____

_____

_____

e　◖●●◗　Explain how Wilkinson's Window Tinting may have applied the principles of Lewin's Force Field Analysis when purchasing the new machinery and automating the tinting process.　　　4 marks

_____

_____

_____

_____

_____

_____

_____

_____

_____

_____

# AREA OF STUDY 1
## TEST 9: REVIEWING PERFORMANCE – THE NEED FOR CHANGE

**Instructions to students**
- Answer **all** questions in the spaces provided

**Total marks:** 30
**Suggested time:** 45 mins

©VCAA 2021 SB Q1 AND 2 PARAPHRASED

CASE STUDY

Handy Dandies is a service business providing nannies and nurses for private residential care. Established in the early 2000s, the partners entered the home care market at a time of peak demand, so their business quickly expanded. As part of the regular evaluation cycle, data has been collected to determine the current state of the business. The following key performance indicator (KPI) charts have been presented to senior management in order to discuss driving and restraining forces. Some managers argue there is a need to act swiftly to change some concerning trends, while others want to plan a more strategic management approach.

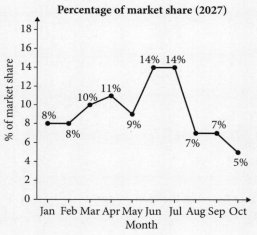

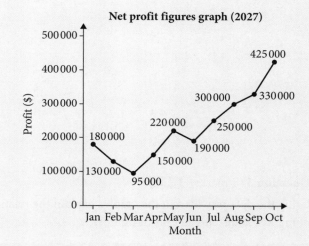

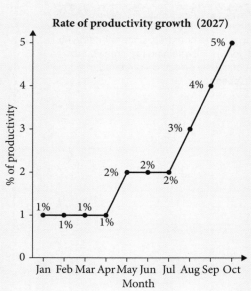

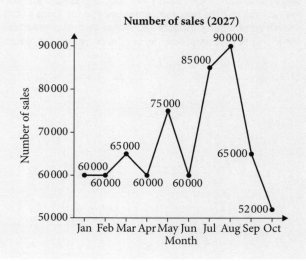

**Question 1** (2 marks) ●○○

Define the term 'key performance indicator'.

_____

_____

_____

_____

**Question 2** (2 marks) ●●○

Explain how a manager might use the key performance indicator 'net profit' to make decisions concerning the future of the business.

| Hint |
| --- |
| Of course, it is always important to read questions carefully and this one is an example of when the nerves during test reading time might cause you to skip over a word here and there. If you focus on the term 'net profit' and miss the words 'how' and 'use', you may simply provide a definition, something that does not attract any marks. Including words and phrases used in the question in your response will keep you on track. |

_____

_____

_____

_____

_____

**Question 3** (3 marks) ●●○

Using the data provided in the graphs, explain the relationship between the 'percentage of market share' and 'net profit figures'.

| Hint |
| --- |
| Explaining the relationship between two concepts involves using the terms in ways that show you understand what they mean. Short definitions may help, but you can also demonstrate understanding by the way you use the terms in sentences and the kinds of examples you use. Explaining requires you to show how one thing impacts another, or, as in this case, has no direct causal effect. Be prepared to go either way in your response, depending on your close reading of the scenario. |

_____

_____

_____

_____

_____

_____

**Question 4** (2 marks)

Define the term 'reactive approach'.

> **Hint**
> Although you can state how one term is the opposite of another in a response, simply stating that is not enough to show you understand what either term means. Ensure you give examples that make business sense. Top answers link examples with the stimulus material.

**Question 5** (3 marks)

Propose and justify a proactive management response with reference to the 'rate of productivity growth' data.

**Question 6** (7 marks)

a    Other than those mentioned in the graphs, identify and explain a relevant key performance indicator Handy Dandies might use to make decisions.    3 marks

**b** ⬤⬤⬤ Predict and justify where the key performance indicator (identified in question 6a) might trend next in relation to the information given.

4 marks

> **Hint**
> When faced with an opinion question that has no right answer, one mark might be a 'give'; however, higher marks are allocated on demonstrated understanding, level of detail and close links to the stimulus material or, where suitable, another relevant business example. Remember to always clearly state WHY you have suggested something, and check the number of allocated marks to determine how long your answer needs to be or the number of points you need to make. You are allowed to make educated guesses, as long as you back them up with explanations for your choices.

_____

_____

_____

_____

_____

_____

_____

_____

_____

_____

_____

_____

**Question 7** (2 marks) ⬤⬤⬤

Outline how a manager might use Lewin's Force Field Analysis theory in relation to 'ranking'.

> **Hint**
> Although it is preferable to link to a provided case study where possible, you may find a question pops up in a test that does not specifically ask for a link. In that case, check the marks carefully as you may be able to work out whether it is expected to have examples suitable for the business scenario. A low-mark question may just require a general response. If you are unsure, the best course of action is to link to the case study so that you can be confident all expectations have been addressed.

_____

_____

_____

_____

_____

**Question 8** (5 marks) ⚫⚫▪

Distinguish between driving and restraining forces with reference to the data related
to the percentage of market share.

**Hint**

Paragraphs are not required, but can help you to stay on track and answer all parts of a question. Note
that you can't flip a factor or force without an explanation of how the situation differs in each case. For
example, you can't say managers may be both driving and restraining forces without giving detail that
clearly shows how that might happen.

**Question 9** (4 marks) ⬤⬤◻

Discuss whether Handy Dandies should approach strategic management according to Porter's Generic Strategy of 'differentiation'.

_____

_____

_____

_____

_____

_____

_____

_____

_____

_____

_____

# AREA OF STUDY 2
# TEST 10: IMPLEMENTING CHANGE

| Instructions to students | | Total marks: | 30 |
|---|---|---|---|
| • Answer **all** questions in the spaces provided | | Suggested time: | 45 mins |

**Question 1** (2 marks)

State **two** potential outcomes for a business of having an ineffective leader during change.

_____

_____

_____

_____

_____

**Question 2** (4 marks)

Suggest and justify **two** ways a business might seek new business opportunities globally.

_____

_____

_____

_____

_____

_____

_____

_____

_____

_____

**Question 3** (3 marks) ⚫⚫⚫

Distinguish between low-risk strategies and high-risk strategies to overcome employee
resistance to change.

_____

_____

_____

_____

_____

_____

_____

_____

**Question 4** (4 marks) ⚫⚫⚫

Analyse the potential effects of increased investment in technology on managers.

_____

_____

_____

_____

_____

_____

_____

_____

_____

_____

_____

**Question 5** (13 marks)

©VCAA  2020 SB CASE STUDY STIMULUS (PART OF)

CASE STUDY

Below is an extract of a speech delivered to the shareholders of Manitta Mining by its Chief Executive Officer at its annual general meeting on 7 August 2020.

As Chief Executive Officer of Manitta Mining for more than 15 years, I am pleased to tell you the long-term outlook for the company remains strong. Since the appointment of a new operations manager, Dr Margaret Sherckle, in February 2020, the number of workplace accidents has decreased by 25%. The number of workplace accidents is a very important key performance indicator (KPI) for the business and a key business objective is to improve workplace safety.

Manitta Mining currently has more than 20 000 employees, each of whom I consider to be part of the 'Manitta family'. While business efficiency and effectiveness are important, the goal of ensuring that our employees return home safely each day is our priority.

**a** ©VCAA 2020 SB Q3 ●● Explain how Manitta Mining could apply each of the steps of the Three-step Change Model (Lewin) to reduce the number of workplace accidents.     6 marks

**Hint**

Watch out for normal English use of words – this is an 'explain' question, meaning you must illustrate cause and effect, but it also asks how something might be 'applied' in real life. So, essentially, you do have to show how to apply facets of the theory, but to meet the expectations of 'explain' you must also demonstrate why applying the theory is a good idea.

When applying theory to a given case study or business scenario, remember to use pieces from the stimulus to show you understand how the scenario would play out in a real-life business sense. Remember, if any business name can be substituted in your answer and it still makes sense, then you have not earned any marks for that point as you have not been specific enough.

**b**  ◖◖◗  Examine how Manitta Mining might respond to the key performance indicator 'number of workplace accidents' through increased investment in staff training.          3 marks

_____

_____

_____

_____

_____

_____

_____

_____

_____

**c**  ©VCAA  2020 SB Q5  ◖◖◗  Explain the importance for Manitta Mining of reviewing its KPIs when evaluating the effectiveness of business transformation.          4 marks

_____

_____

_____

_____

_____

_____

_____

_____

_____

_____

_____

_____

**Question 6** (4 marks) ⬤⬤⬤

Give a real-life example that you have studied this year to discuss corporate social responsibility considerations when implementing change.

> **Hint**
> When asked to use a real-life example, you may use any you have studied or personally have knowledge of or have interacted with. The expectation is that you show why the business you have suggested fits the criteria of the question.

---------------------------------------------------------------

---------------------------------------------------------------

---------------------------------------------------------------

---------------------------------------------------------------

---------------------------------------------------------------

---------------------------------------------------------------

---------------------------------------------------------------

---------------------------------------------------------------

---------------------------------------------------------------

---------------------------------------------------------------

# AREA OF STUDY 2
## TEST 11: IMPLEMENTING CHANGE

**Instructions to students**
- Answer **all** questions in the spaces provided

**Total marks:** 30
**Suggested time:** 45 mins

**CASE STUDY**

Lakeside Health is a small medical clinic that has been operating for 20 years and is owned by partners Oscar and Aroha. Lakeside Health has four general practitioners, two nurses and five administration team members. The clinic operates an internal computer system and has a basic website; however, Oscar and Aroha have become concerned that their reluctance to introduce new technologies is affecting the performance of the business, based on the data shown in the table.

Following the appointment of a new administration manager, Oscar and Aroha plan to introduce a new website with an interactive online booking system, SMS appointment reminders and on-demand telehealth services. They are also considering the purchase of new diagnostic equipment and a renovation of the premises to modernise facilities. While they are excited about the future of the clinic, they are worried about the impact that these changes will have on their clinic's culture and employee morale.

| Key performance indicator | 2025 | 2026 | 2027 |
|---|---|---|---|
| Net profit figures | $135 000 | $121 500 | $115 800 |
| Number of website hits | 2510 | 2290 | 1990 |
| Total number of appointments | 20 800 | 19 775 | 18 680 |
| Level of staff turnover | 7% | 5% | 15% |

**Question 1** (2 marks)

Define the term 'corporate culture'.

_____

_____

_____

_____

_____

**Question 2** (3 marks) ⬤⬤⬤

Propose and justify **one** strategy Oscar and Aroha can implement to improve corporate culture at Lakeside Health.

_____

_____

_____

_____

_____

_____

_____

**Question 3** (6 marks) ⬤⬤⬜

Explain how Oscar and Aroha can apply **two** of the principles of Senge's Learning Organisation to create a positive culture for change.

> **Hint**
> When selecting the two principles to include in your response, ensure that you select the principles you know well and for which you can make relevant and logical links to the stimulus material.

_____

_____

_____

_____

_____

_____

_____

_____

_____

_____

_____

_____

_____

**Question 4** (4 marks)

With reference to the data provided, explain the importance of leadership during this period of change at Lakeside Health.

_____

_____

_____

_____

_____

_____

_____

_____

_____

_____

_____

**Question 5** (4 marks)

Compare the potential effects of change on the employees and customers of Lakeside Health.

_____

_____

_____

_____

_____

_____

_____

_____

_____

_____

_____

**Question 6** (5 marks)

Evaluate the use of empowerment as a low-risk strategy to overcome employee resistance to the introduction of new technologies and renovation of the premises.

**Hint**

Ensure that you support your opinion in your conclusion by reiterating your strongest arguments, whether for or against the use of empowerment.

**Question 7** (6 marks)

Describe how each of the following strategies could be used to respond to the key performance indicators, presented in the table at the start of the test, in order to improve business performance in the future.

**a** Improving quality in production 3 marks

**b** Staff training 3 marks

# AREAS OF STUDY 1–2
## TEST 12: UNIT 4

| Instructions to students | Total marks: 60 |
|---|---|
| • Answer **all** questions in the spaces provided | Suggested time: 45 mins |

**Question 1** (25 marks)

> **CASE STUDY**
>
> Alliance Real Estate is a real estate agency based in a large town in central Victoria. Changes in the external environment have led to a significant increase in demand for regional and rural properties, often from clients who are based in Melbourne, interstate or overseas. In response to this demand and to gain competitive advantage, the owners of Alliance Real Estate have invested in a range of innovative technologies to enable clients to purchase property online, including 3D inspection technology, a virtual furnishing app, an online sales platform and digital contract completion software.
>
> These changes have resulted in a range of operational changes, including the development of new job descriptions for the sales team and the administration team, a change in office layout and the increased need for training.

a   ◖●◗◗   Describe how Alliance Real Estate could use the following key performance indicators to measure business performance.

    i   Number of website hits                                            2 marks

    ii   Percentage of market share                                   2 marks

**b**   ⚫◯◯   Outline how Alliance Real Estate has sought new business opportunities through the redeployment of capital or labour resources.                    2 marks

> **Hint**
> When you are given the choice of two possible strategies to write about, choose the strategy about which you feel most confident writing and making clear links back to the stimulus materials provided.

_____

_____

_____

_____

_____

_____

**c**   ⚫⚫◯   Explain how Alliance Real Estate might apply the principles of Lewin's Force Field Analysis to take advantage of new business opportunities.                    4 marks

_____

_____

_____

_____

_____

_____

_____

_____

_____

_____

**d** ▮◌◌▮ Other than pursuit of profit, explain **two** driving forces that might have influenced change at Alliance Real Estate.      4 marks

_____

_____

_____

_____

_____

_____

_____

_____

_____

_____

**e** ▮◌◌◌▮ Evaluate the effect of the changes at Alliance Real Estate on the general community.      5 marks

_____

_____

_____

_____

_____

_____

_____

_____

_____

_____

_____

_____

_____

**f** ⬤⬤⬤ There are a number of employees who are not happy with the changes that have been implemented. Propose and justify **one** low-risk and **one** high-risk strategy to overcome employee resistance to change.     6 marks

> **Hint**
>
> When selecting your strategies, think about which strategies from the Study Design make the most sense for a real estate business where the majority of revenue is generated by earning commission on the sale of properties. The strategies used by a real estate business are likely to be different to those used by a manufacturing business or social enterprise.

---
---
---
---
---
---
---
---
---
---
---
---
---

**Question 2** (10 marks) ©VCAA 2019 SA Q4 ●●●

Leaders can inspire change within a business. Analyse how managers can apply the principles of Senge's Learning Organisation during a period of change, in order to:

- effectively manage employees
- positively influence corporate culture
- ensure the change is implemented successfully.

> **Hint**
> Using paragraphs in an extended response signals to the assessor how you have addressed all aspects of the question by grouping your key ideas and points of analysis/application.

**Question 3** (25 marks)   ©VCAA   2017 SB CASE STUDY STIMULUS

The following is the first page from the 2017 'Report to Shareholders' of Shandra's Dairy Ltd.

CASE STUDY

Commencing as a family-run business 15 years ago, we are now one of the largest independent dairies in Australia. We are proud of the fact that our raw materials are sourced from local suppliers and that customer satisfaction remains at the centre of our operations. We use a strict quality control strategy to maintain the overall excellence of our products.

**Business highlights in 2017**
- Market share increased from 15% to 17%
- Increase in volumes of sales to over 10 million litres of ice-cream
- Installation of four modern wind turbines at a total cost of $1.25 million, reducing carbon emissions by 3500 tonnes per year, thus assisting us in meeting our 2020 renewable energy target
- A saving of $500 000 per year on electricity bills due to the installation of 600 solar panels

One of our key objectives is to enhance levels of environmental sustainability and make our entire site self-sufficient through renewable energy. Our CEO, Johanna Taylor, is eager to ensure that over 23% of the electricity used comes from renewable sources by 2020. This fits in with the Australian Government's Renewable Energy Target.

'Our commitment to renewable energy has meant an increase in expenses and debt in the short term, but shareholders will continue to see value as the saving in electricity costs will be sustained into the future.'

—Johanna Taylor

Another objective is to become a truly global brand – to do this we need to diversify. Our aim is to launch into the snack food market, concentrating on potato chips. These can be produced at our present manufacturing plant and with the use of our existing suppliers. We believe that this could commence by 2020 and we could export to markets in over 20 countries.

**Future goals**
- Implement a second strategy to improve quality by 1 July 2018
- Diversify into the snack food market within the next three years

**a** Describe the concept of business change for Shandra's Dairy Ltd.    2 marks

b  ●● ▇  Using evidence from the case study, identify and explain whether Shandra's Dairy
Ltd is taking a proactive or reactive approach to change.                                          4 marks

> **Hint**
> Because three of the marks are allocated to the inclusion of supporting evidence, including three
> distinctive examples from the case study will help to maximise the marks awarded to support
> an explanation.

_____

_____

_____

_____

_____

_____

_____

_____

_____

_____

_____

c  ●○○ ▇  In relation to environmental sustainability, describe **two** strategies the managers
of Shandra's Dairy Ltd could implement to strengthen corporate culture.                            4 marks

> **Hint**
> The Study Design does not list strategies to strengthen corporate culture, so it is important to prepare
> for questions with a range of business scenarios and case studies, and by including a comprehensive
> list of strategies in your study notes gleaned from multiple sources.

_____

_____

_____

_____

_____

_____

_____

_____

_____

_____

_____

**d** ©VCAA 2017 SB Q4 MODIFIED ⬤⬤⬜ Shandra's Dairy Ltd wants to diversify into the snack food market within the next three years. Apply Lewin's Three-step Change Model to assist Shandra's Dairy Ltd with this future goal. Explain how organisational inertia and financial considerations may act as restraining forces against Shandra's Dairy Ltd becoming a truly global brand.

10 marks

**Hint**
To gain full marks for this question, you need to provide logical examples of how each step would be applied for Shandra's Dairy Ltd to successfully diversify into the snack food market.

_____

_____

_____

e  ©VCAA  2017 SB Q5  ●● Identify **one** of the key approaches to strategic management
from Porter's Generic Strategies. Discuss how this approach could be applied in relation
to Shandra's Dairy Ltd.                                                   5 marks

_____

_____

_____

_____

_____

_____

_____

_____

_____

_____

_____

_____

_____

_____

_____

_____

SAMPLE

STUDENT NUMBER

**Letter**

# BUSINESS MANAGEMENT

## Written examination

Reading time: 15 minutes

Writing time: 2 hours

### QUESTION AND ANSWER BOOK

#### Structure of book

| Section | Number of questions | Number of questions to be answered | Marks |
|---------|---------------------|-----------------------------------|-------|
| A | 4 | 4 | 40 |
| B | 7 | 7 | 35 |
| | | Total | 75 |

- Students are permitted to bring into the examination room: pens, pencils, highlighters, erasers, sharpeners and rulers.
- Students are NOT permitted to bring into the examination room: blank sheets of paper and/or correction fluid/tape.
- No calculator is allowed in this examination.

**Materials supplied**
- Question and answer book of 16 pages.
- Additional space is available at the end of this exam if you need extra space to complete an answer.

**Instructions**
- Write your **student number** in the space provided above on this page.
- All written responses must be in English.

**Students are NOT permitted to bring mobile phones and/or any other unauthorised electronic devices into the examination room.**

# Section A

**Instructions for Section A**
- Answer **all** questions in the spaces provided

**Question 1** (17 marks)

*Go for it* is a podcast, online training and online coaching business run by sole trader, Sarah Shine. Sarah works from home and has been working by herself for the past 3 years. Due to a 60% increase in sales over the past 6 months, Sarah has decided to grow her business by employing a marketing consultant and virtual assistant to work 20 hours per week.

**a**    Outline the business characteristics of a sole trader like Sarah.    2 marks

_____

_____

_____

_____

_____

_____

_____

**b**    Other than 'number of sales', describe **two** key performance indicators that would be relevant to a business like *Go for it*.    4 marks

_____

_____

_____

_____

_____

_____

_____

_____

_____

_____

_____

_____

*Question 1 continues on page 71*

**c** Through an online freelancing platform, Sarah has found an impressive virtual assistant candidate located in Brazil. However, Sarah feels conflicted about hiring someone who is not from her local community.

Discuss the considerations Sarah needs to take into account in relation to global outsourcing.     4 marks

**d** Propose and justify an appropriate management style Sarah can use when building a team that will work remotely.     4 marks

*Question 1 continues on page 72*

**e** Assess the suitability of on-the-job training for new employees at *Go for it*. 3 marks

_____

_____

_____

_____

_____

_____

_____

_____

_____

_____

**Question 2** (6 marks)

**a** Describe the concept of business change. 2 marks

_____

_____

_____

_____

_____

_____

_____

*Question 2 continues on page 73*

**b**   Compare 'manipulation' and 'threat' as strategies to overcome employee resistance to change.          4 marks

_____

_____

_____

_____

_____

_____

_____

_____

_____

_____

_____

_____

_____

*End of Question 2*

**Question 3** (6 marks)

With reference to a contemporary case study, analyse the use of artificial intelligence to improve the efficiency and effectiveness of operations.

_____

_____

_____

_____

_____

_____

_____

_____

_____

_____

_____

_____

_____

_____

_____

_____

_____

_____

_____

_____

_____

*End of Question 3*

**Question 4** (11 marks)

Chow Chow is a restaurant chain owned by partners Baylee and Kim, with seven locations in Victoria. The owners are planning to expand by opening eight new locations, along the east coast of Australia, over the next 3 years. The average rate of staff absenteeism has increased from 4 days to 10 days in the past year.

**a**   Explain the role of the human resource manager at Chow Chow.                                           3 marks

_____

_____

_____

_____

_____

_____

_____

_____

_____

_____

_Question 4 continues on page 76_

**b**    Concerned about the increase in staff absenteeism, Baylee and Kim have asked the human resource manager to implement initiatives to address this issue, including application of the Four Drive Theory and implementation of strategies to improve motivation. Apply the Four Drive Theory of motivation at Chow Chow.    4 marks

_____

_____

_____

_____

_____

_____

_____

_____

_____

_____

_____

_____

_____

_____

_Question 4 continues on page 77_

c    Outline how career advancement can be used to improve short-term and long-term motivation
at Chow Chow.

4 marks

*End of Question 4*

# Section B – Case study

**Instructions for Section B**
- Use the case study provided to answer the questions in this section. Answers must apply to the case study.
- Answer **all** questions in the spaces provided

## CASE STUDY

Radlee Pty Ltd is an award-winning manufacturer of lightweight, carbon fibre mountain bikes. Radlee Pty Ltd holds the patent for an innovative suspension system, which it manufactures in its state-of-the-art manufacturing facility in Dandenong, Victoria. Production involves the combination of an automated production line, robotics and highly skilled engineers. The mountain bike frames, tyres, seats and handlebars are manufactured in China, shipped to Australia monthly and delivered directly to Dandenong. The bikes are assembled in Dandenong and delivered to Australian retailers or directly to online customers purchasing from the Radlee Pty Ltd website. Demand for mountain bikes peaks during spring and in the lead-up to Christmas. Currently, 10% of stock is exported to the United States (US).

The owners have reviewed the performance of Radlee Pty Ltd over the past 2 years.

| Key performance indicator | January–June 2026 | July–December 2026 | January–June 2027 | July–December 2027 |
|---|---|---|---|---|
| Number of sales | 1287 units | 1332 units | 1231 units | 1315 units |
| Level of waste | 5% | 3% | 6% | 4% |
| Number of workplace accidents | 10 | 8 | 8 | 13 |

Future goals for Radlee Pty Ltd include:
- increase exports to 25% of total sales by 2030
- improve the management of materials
- reduce waste to consistently 3% or below.

istockphoto.com/branex

**Question 1** (2 marks)

Other than 'to make a profit', outline a relevant business objective for Radlee Pty Ltd.

_____

_____

_____

_____

_____

_____

_____

_____

*End of Question 1*

**Question 2** (3 marks)

With reference to the data provided, propose and justify a materials management strategy to improve the efficiency of operations at Radlee Pty Ltd.

_____

_____

_____

_____

_____

_____

_____

_____

_____

**Question 3** (4 marks)

Explain **one** driving force and **one** restraining force that could impact Radlee Pty Ltd reducing the number of workplace accidents.

_____

_____

_____

_____

_____

_____

_____

_____

_____

_____

_____

_____

_____

_____

_____

_____

_End of Question 3_

**Question 4** (6 marks)

Analyse how **two** of the following management strategies could be used to seek new business opportunities for Radlee Pty Ltd:

- improved quality in production

- redeployment of resources

- cost cutting

- innovation.

*End of Question 4*

**Question 5** (10 marks)

The objectives of Radlee Pty Ltd must cater to the needs of all stakeholders.

Analyse this statement with reference to:

- the interests of stakeholders
- potential conflicts between stakeholders
- the effect of change on stakeholder groups.

*Question 5 continues on page 82*

_____

_____

_____

_____

_____

_____

_____

_____

_____

_____

_____

_____

_____

_____

**Question 6** (6 marks)

Discuss the use of the differentiation approach to increase exports to 25% by 2030.

_____

_____

_____

_____

_____

_____

_____

_____

_____

_____

*Question 6 continues on page 83*

**Question 7** (4 marks)

Describe why it is important for Radlee Pty Ltd to consider corporate social responsibility when implementing change in the future.

**END OF PAPER**

**SECTION B EXTRA WORKING SPACE**

SAMPLE

STUDENT NUMBER

Letter

# BUSINESS MANAGEMENT

## Written examination

Reading time: 15 minutes

Writing time: 2 hours

## QUESTION AND ANSWER BOOK

### Structure of book

| Section | Number of questions | Number of questions to be answered | Marks |
|---------|---------------------|-----------------------------------|-------|
| A | 5 | 5 | 50 |
| B | 6 | 6 | 25 |
| | | Total | 75 |

- Students are permitted to bring into the examination room: pens, pencils, highlighters, erasers, sharpeners and rulers.
- Students are NOT permitted to bring into the examination room: blank sheets of paper and/or correction fluid/tape.
- No calculator is allowed in this examination.

**Materials supplied**
- Question and answer book of 18 pages.
- Additional space is available at the end of this exam if you need extra space to complete an answer.

**Instructions**
- Write your **student number** in the space provided above on this page.
- All written responses must be in English.

**Students are NOT permitted to bring mobile phones and/or any other unauthorised electronic devices into the examination room.**

# Section A

Instructions for Section A
· Answer **all** questions in the spaces provided

**Question 1** (15 marks)

AssetArt Pty Ltd is owned by graphic designers Birrani and Max. AssetArt Pty Ltd specialises in designing, producing and selling graphics, in the form of non-fungible tokens (NFTs). Due to unexpected and rapid expansion of the business, arising from high global demand for NFTs, Birrani and Max have hired 30 new staff in the past 12 months, including a human resource manager to manage employees more effectively.

**a**  Define the term 'human resource management'.    2 marks

_____

_____

_____

_____

_____

_____

_____

**b**  Outline the relationship between human resources and the business objective 'to fulfil a market need' at AssetArt Pty Ltd.    3 marks

_____

_____

_____

_____

_____

_____

_____

_____

_____

*Question 1 continues on page 87*

c    After speaking with employees, the human resource manager has found that recently recruited senior artists and graphic designers feel like their skills and experience are being overlooked and underutilised. A number of them are already considering job opportunities elsewhere. The human resource manager has told the partners they need to delegate more to the senior employees, but Birrani and Max feel unsure about how to do this.

Discuss the use of the management skill of 'delegation' at AssetArt Pty Ltd.                 4 marks

_Question 1 continues on page 88_

**d** Pay and conditions at AssetArt are currently determined by the Graphic Arts, Printing and Publishing Award 2022. The human resource manager has recommended the business change to an agreement.

Describe **two** differences between an award and an agreement. Analyse the extent to which you agree or disagree with the recommendation made by the human resource manager.

6 marks

_____

_____

_____

_____

_____

_____

_____

_____

_____

_____

_____

_____

_____

_____

_____

_____

_____

_____

_____

_____

*End of Question 1*

**Question 2** (5 marks)

With reference to a contemporary case study, apply the principles of Lewin's Force Field Analysis.

*End of Question 2*

**Question 3** (9 marks)

a    Distinguish between official and real corporate culture.                    3 marks

_____

_____

_____

_____

_____

_____

_____

_____

_____

_____

_____

_____

_____

_____

_____

_____

_____

_____

_____

_____

_____

_____

_____

_____

*Question 3 continues on page 91*

**b** Propose and justify **two** strategies to develop corporate culture for a business that is introducing robotics into the production process.

6 marks

*End of Question 3*

**Question 4** (10 marks)

'Competition brings out the best in products and the worst in people.' — David Sarnoff, Founder, US National Broadcasting Co. Inc.

Evaluate this statement.

*Question 4 continues on page 93*

**Question 5** (11 marks)

Topperz is an online business that specialises in personalised cake toppers and party signs. As the sole proprietor of Topperz, Kate works from home and has her computer and 3D printing equipment set up in her garage. She receives orders from her website 24 hours a day, 7 days a week, and finds it difficult to meet high demand quickly. She has reviewed her key performance indicators over the past year to discover that the number of sales has increased by 15%, but net profit has only increased by 3%. Kate feels like she wastes a lot of time and resources in the way she operates and has been researching the concept of lean management.

a   Other than those identified in the scenario above, outline **one** key performance indicator Kate can use to analyse business performance.

2 marks

*Question 5 continues on page 94*

**b**  Analyse how initiating lean production techniques may help Kate respond to key
performance indicators.

4 marks

_____

_____

_____

_____

_____

_____

_____

_____

_____

_____

_____

_____

_____

**c**  Kate has noticed increased requests for customised party packages to include products such as
invitations, balloons, cupcake decorations and bunting. She is considering how to broaden the range
of products sold by Topperz, but currently only has equipment to make cake toppers and party signs.

Describe how Kate might use global sourcing of inputs to expand her product range.

2 marks

_____

_____

_____

_____

_____

_____

_____

_Question 5 continues on page 95_

**d**   Explain **one** corporate social responsibility consideration that may influence Kate's decisions about using global sourcing of inputs.

3 marks

_End of Question 5_

# Section B – Case study

**CASE STUDY**
Extract of a newspaper article, published in the *Central Gazette*, 12 November 2027

# Building a Comfy Community

Comfy Community is a rare gem, nestled in the Central Victorian bush. The brainchild of partners Rock and Zan, Comfy Community is a village of tiny houses, built for older women experiencing homelessness or financial difficulties. A social enterprise, Comfy Community started as two cottages built on Rock and Zan's 20-acre property in 2021 during the COVID-19 pandemic. It is now home to 120 residents, a community centre, an apple orchard and 58 tiny houses in total.

shutterstock.com/ branislavpudar

'We couldn't have done it without the support of the local and global community', explains Zan. 'Through a combination of crowdfunding, financial support from our local bank, a range of grants from the government and donations of time, money, resources and skills from generous people in our local community, including our wonderful neighbours, we have been able to achieve our vision of creating a nurturing space for people to rebuild their lives after experiencing hardship.'

Comfy Community residents pay a weekly amount that covers rent, utilities and access to the community centre, with 100% of profits going back into maintaining the community and funding new business ventures. The community centre currently offers onsite services such as digital literacy and woodworking classes, financial support services and a wellness gym.

'We are excited to announce that our new general store and childcare centre will be opening to the general public on 1 December this year', announces Rock. 'We are committed to providing a safe, supportive and sustainable community for our residents, and part of delivering on that commitment involves being entrepreneurial. The vision is for our Comfy Community to embrace new business opportunities, through providing a range of goods and services to the broader community.'

Zan and Rock have employed a number of Comfy Community residents to staff the new facilities. Millie has been a resident for 3 years and is excited about starting her new job as the manager of the general store.

'When I first came to Comfy Community, I had not worked in over 15 years. Zan and Rock offered me a job in the community centre and now I've worked my way up to manager. I can't believe this is my life now!', exclaims Millie.

'It hasn't always been easy', explains Rock. 'There have been times we couldn't get finance, or had delays with planning permits for various stages of the build, but somehow we've always managed to pull together to overcome obstacles. Our determination has paid off. In the past 2 years, our business operations have been profitable and we are less reliant on outside investment.'

So, what is next for the Comfy Community? Opening a bakery, of course!

'Some of our residents have been baking delicious goodies using apples from the orchard and selling them at local markets, with most market days selling out within an hour or two. We can't keep up with demand', says Zan. 'The Comfy Bakehouse is already under construction and should be open to the public in April next year.'

**Question 1** (2 marks)

Outline the features of a social enterprise like Comfy Community.

**Question 2** (4 marks)

Compare the characteristics of the operations of the community centre and the bakehouse at Comfy Community.

*End of Question 2*

**Question 3** (4 marks)

Describe **one** driving force and **one** restraining force that has influenced change at Comfy Community.

_____

_____

_____

_____

_____

_____

_____

_____

_____

_____

_____

_____

_____

*End of Question 3*

**Question 4** (6 marks)

Apply the principles of Senge's Learning Organisation to create and maintain a positive culture for change at Comfy Community.

_End of Question 4_

**Question 5** (4 marks)

Rock and Zan are seeking to implement a quality management strategy across all business operations at Comfy Community.

Discuss the use of Total Quality Management to improve the effectiveness of operations at Comfy Community.

_____

_____

_____

_____

_____

_____

_____

_____

_____

_____

_____

_____

_____

*End of Question 5*

**Question 6** (5 marks)

Describe whether Rock and Zan are taking a proactive or reactive approach to change. Use examples from the case study to justify your response.

_____

_____

_____

_____

_____

_____

_____

_____

_____

_____

_____

_____

_____

_____

_____

**END OF PAPER**

**SECTION B EXTRA WORKING SPACE**

# SOLUTIONS

## TEST 1: BUSINESS FOUNDATIONS

### Question 1

Corporate culture is the values and beliefs published by the organisation (official) and demonstrated by employees of the organisation through their behaviours at work (real). For example, workers choosing to correctly use a recycling process demonstrates a corporate culture that values sustainability.

The response gives a valid characteristic that demonstrates corporate culture and an example to illustrate what corporate culture looks like in practice.

As there are only two marks available, there is no requirement to mention official and real corporate culture, although you can if you wish. Test reading time should allow you to note that this is what the next question is about, so you might choose to save this information for question 2.

**Mark breakdown:**
- 1 mark for giving correct characteristic(s) of corporate culture
- 1 mark for detail or appropriate example

### Question 2

Official corporate culture refers to expectations an organisation publishes, such as in policies, set processes and marketing communications, whereas real corporate culture is how the employees actually behave day to day while working. The difference is that official culture involves business directives or guidelines; however, these are not necessarily what employees follow if they take shortcuts for efficiency, when not in the public eye or when there is little supervision.

This high-scoring response demonstrates understanding of both terms by giving examples of relevant behaviours and explicitly highlights a key difference between the two terms.

**Mark breakdown:**
- 1 mark for showing understanding of official corporate culture
- 1 mark for showing understanding of real corporate culture
- 1 mark for showing the difference between official and real corporate culture

**Top tip**

There is a difference between a 'strong' corporate culture (where everyone does the same thing) and a 'weak' corporate culture (where everyone does what they want). However, this does not in any way equate with the use of different strict or casual management styles, as either could have the same result. It also doesn't link to 'official' and 'real' culture, because you could have a strong 'real' culture, where most workers take shortcuts, or a weak 'official' culture, where workers do not follow directives. Read the questions carefully to work out exactly what is being asked.

### Question 3

**a** A business partnership, made up of 2 to 20 people, may be chosen instead of being a sole trader, because with more than one owner there may be more financial capital and business expertise to draw on. A sole trader structure means the owner must finance the business on their own, so a partnership may be a better choice, whereby all partners have loan capabilities with access to more varied and extensive financial resources.

This response snuck in a short definition to demonstrate understanding of the terms. While not strictly required, it does show a high knowledge level and, when formatted in this way, really only takes a short time to write using little line space. Unless specifically asked, you can decide when you think this is appropriate as there are no marks allocated for definitions.

However, as 'rather than a sole trader' is part of the question, you are expected to briefly show a link or comparison between the two business structures, with reference to the point being made.

Further reasons could be shared workload, business perpetuity or shared decision-making; however, there are no marks allocated for any extra reasons given, other than the one detailed.

For further detail on this past examination question, see the *2017 VCE Business Management examination report* on the VCAA website.

**Mark breakdown:**
- 1 mark for providing some detail about an appropriate reason to operate as a partnership
- 1 mark for linking given reason to operating as a sole trader

**b** A disadvantage of the partnership structure is that partners must share any business profits in accordance with their percentage of ownership. This means less return on their capital investment and less monetary compensation for their work than if they were a sole trader, where they would receive 100% of business profit after paying costs.

This response gives a disadvantage and then provides some detail, including a brief comparison with a sole trader situation. It also sneaks in a comment to demonstrate an understanding of how profit is calculated.

As in question 3a, you might include some extra disadvantages here to practise stretching your memory muscles (e.g. unlimited liability). However, once again you won't get any marks for doing so. Be very careful not to waste test time on unmarked components or use up lines writing extra information, as you might mistakenly think you've answered all parts of the question because your page looks full.

**Mark breakdown:**
- 1 mark for demonstrating understanding of a negative aspect of operating as a partnership
- 1 mark for detail or an appropriate example

## Question 4

**a** One type of business is a social enterprise, where profits contribute to social improvements or society's wellbeing. *The Big Issue* is an example of a social enterprise, because profits made from selling magazines go back not only to improve the organisation, but also to the individual, mostly homeless magazine sellers, providing some income to improve their situation.

You have had a helping hand to answer this question by answering questions 3a and 3b; however, you will still need to be aware that business structures are also known as business 'types'. Select from sole trader, partnership, private limited company, public listed company, social enterprise or government business enterprise. The 'real-life example' needs to come from an organisation you have studied or from your own personal experience.

**Mark breakdown:**
- 1 mark for stating a type of business listed in the Study Design
- 1 mark for providing a real-life example of the stated type of business

**b** As a social enterprise, an appropriate business objective for *The Big Issue* would be fulfilling a social need. For example, this organisation may aim to improve the work skills and housing situation of the magazine sellers. They might fulfil this objective by training sellers in good customer service, money management and other transferable work skills. They might also fulfill it by allowing sellers to retain a percentage of the profits from their sales, intended as an income to pay for housing, thus improving society overall by helping to avoid homelessness.

As indicated, you must only refer to the same business type mentioned in your response to question 4a. There is no specific requirement type of objective here, so you can use high-level objectives, such as those found in a mission statement, or low-level objectives, such as day-to-day targets.

If you are not sure of the actual objectives of a real example, you can make an educated guess based on their business type. Here, the response uses the words 'may' and 'might' and then gives some appropriate suggestions and justifications. It also returns to the question at the end to ensure relevance.

**Mark breakdown:**
- 1 mark for providing an appropriate business objective for the stated business type
- 1 mark for giving a reason why this objective suits the stated business type

**c** *The Big Issue* stakeholders have a vested interest in the organisation. This includes employees, such as the magazine sellers who purchase products to sell and represent the organisation, and customers, who are the people buying the magazine to read, while supporting the sellers.

> This response states the name of the group of people who would count as stakeholders, but also gives a little detail on what they do in relation to the organisation to prove their connection. Managers, owners, suppliers or the general community might also be mentioned, but only if relevant to the given organisation.
>
> This particular case study has a tricky area where 'employees' would also refer to the onsite staff who provide administration and work training for the magazine sellers. So strictly speaking, the sellers themselves could also be termed 'customers' of the organisation. However, even when categorisation gets tricky, as long as you make your internal reasoning clear and it makes business sense, you will be awarded the marks. That's why a short justification may be needed for clarification.
>
> **Mark breakdown:**
> - 1 mark for naming each appropriate stakeholder person or group (× 2)

**d** There may be potential conflict between the sellers as employees, who are mainly homeless and so are very focused on making as much profit as they can to put towards secure housing, and the customers, who may not realise that the relatively high cost of the magazine includes a commission for the seller. Other, more-aware customers may want to stop and have a chat as they purchase their magazine, in order to support and show respect for the sellers, but the magazine sellers may just want to move on to the next customer as quickly as possible so as not to miss any passers-by when chatting. Both employees and customers need to balance their expectations in order to avoid conflict.

> The extra mark here is for added detail or linking to appropriate perspectives of the stakeholders. The key is to demonstrate an understanding of what each person or group of people likely want or need, and how the two different perspectives might be in opposition.
>
> **Mark breakdown:**
> - 1 mark for representing each stakeholder's likely perspective (× 2)
> - 1 mark for providing extra detail such as appropriate source(s) of conflict

## Question 5

Having interpersonal skills means a manager is able to relate well to others and develop professional networks. Managers with high-level interpersonal skills are able to make the kinds of personal connections and shared understandings that make employees feel welcome and valued. This can result in higher worker productivity and stronger staff loyalty, leading to longer staff retention.

> This response defines the term by outlining what it means in practice to have the skill. The added detail illustrates how having the skill can have a positive impact on a business.
>
> **Mark breakdown:**
> - 1 mark for giving the correct characteristic(s) of interpersonal management skills
> - 1 mark for detail such as relevant behaviours, relevant consequences or an appropriate example

## Question 6

Without effective communication skills, a manager might find their employees have little understanding of what workers are expected to be doing or why. This may mean employees are less productive because they are not clear on tasks or how to follow the organisation's policies or procedures, or they may make errors that cause defective products or lead to poor customer service or unsafe work practices. A likely impact of poor communication is employees feeling insecure in their work as they are not clear on or confident about expectations. This may result in workers not attempting tasks they don't understand, getting hurt or leaving, thus adding to staff turnover and associated recruitment costs.

It is important to refer to the impact on employees as that is a question specification. However, for added detail, this response also mentioned the relevant impacts on the business.

**Mark breakdown:**
- 1 mark for stating an appropriate impact on employees
- 2 marks for details, such as consequences for employees or further impacts on the business

## Question 7

As employees are experienced, it would be appropriate to use a laissez-faire management style, whereby workers are set targets and then left to meet standards without close supervision. This would be effective because experienced workers already know and follow business systems, so they don't need monitoring or frequent support. In fact, laissez-faire could be the best management style to use, as experienced staff may resent close supervision and be more productive if they feel valued and respected as experts by being empowered to achieve the set goals in their own way.

This response acknowledges the employee perspective and the benefits for the business of using the selected style. This question reminds us to pay close attention to endings, as the word 'experienced' is a vital component that gives a clue to which style would work best (in this case consultative, participative or laissez-faire), and must be specifically mentioned in any high-scoring response.

**Mark breakdown:**
- 1 mark for naming an appropriate management style
- 1 mark for demonstrating why the stated style is a suitable choice
- 1 mark for detail, such as appropriate management behaviours in this scenario

**Top tip**
You need to be able to do more than just remember the different management styles for the Unit 3 Area of Study 1 outcome; you will be asked to relate the styles to management skills and/or corporate culture in an analysis question. Note that all styles can be effective, depending on the situation, and that good managers are able to call on the appropriate style to deal with a suitable issue.

## Question 8

Managers may be very good at some skills, but may need to better develop others. A successful autocratic manager may be very good at decision-making, giving their workers confidence to follow clear directives. However, an autocratic manager may prefer to keep close control rather than handing over responsibility, meaning they need to further develop their delegation skills. Not delegating becomes an issue when there is more work than can be physically done by one person. So although they retain overall responsibility, managers must learn to select the right employee for the right job and then allow them to do it. This will ensure that the required work gets done, as well as empowering employees, resulting in greater job satisfaction that may lead to higher productivity.

This response discusses likely outcomes by mentioning what might happen if an autocratic manager does not delegate and also some results if they do delegate. It also acknowledges that being an autocratic manager can be successful in some ways.

**Mark breakdown:**
- 1 mark for showing how this management style may be linked to this management skill
- 2 marks for detail, such as suggesting a likely impact on the business if the manager does or does not develop the stated skill

**Top tip**
Many management skills by various theorists can be found on the internet. However, only the skills as listed in the Study Design are examinable.

# TEST 2: BUSINESS FOUNDATIONS

## Question 1

Australia Post is a government business enterprise that is owned and operated by the Australian Government with the purpose of providing a community service and to fulfil commercial obligations. Australia Post provides a community service through supplying a postal service for letters and packages within Australia and between Australia and other countries. Through providing high-quality service in an efficient manner for the community, Australia Post fulfils its commercial obligations by increasing the value of assets and achieving returns for its stakeholder, the government.

> This question requires an explanation of the purpose of a government business enterprise (GBE), rather than a definition or outline of the business type. Therefore, the choice of case study is important, as it is through the link between the case study and how the business provides the community service and fulfils commercial obligations that the explanation has sufficient detail to gain full marks.
>
> **Mark breakdown:**
> - 1 mark for referring to an Australian GBE and outlining the ownership structure
> - 1 mark for linking the purpose of the suggested GBE to providing a community service
> - 1 mark for linking the purpose of the suggested GBE to commercial obligations/achieving returns for the government as stakeholder

## Question 2

a   The stakeholders of Beautiful Blooms are individuals or groups who have a vested interest in the activities of the business and will interact with the business. Stakeholders can be within the business (e.g. the owner or employees of Beautiful Blooms) or external to the business (e.g. the customers and suppliers of Beautiful Blooms).

> When a definition is worth two marks, it is important that your definition is detailed and contains at least two distinctive parts, features or characteristics related to the concept. It is likely that to gain full marks you will need to expand on the definition provided in the glossary of your textbook or online resources.
>    For further detail on this past examination question, see the *2021 VCE Business Management examination report* on the VCAA website.
>
> **Mark breakdown:**
> - 2 marks for a detailed definition of the term, including reference to Beautiful Blooms

b   A private limited company is characterised by being an incorporated business, with between 1 and 50 shareholders, whereas a social enterprise is not characterised by the number of owners/shareholders or whether it is incorporated. Both a private limited company and social enterprise have the objective to sell goods and/or services to make a profit. However, a private limited company typically also has the objective to meet shareholder expectations (e.g. through providing a return on investment), whereas a social enterprise will use profits to reinvest in the business and fulfil a social need (e.g. a community or environmental need).

   Both a private limited company and a social enterprise can have high operating costs. However, for a social enterprise these costs can be different to conventional business expenses (e.g. incurring costs associated with providing services to disadvantaged communities). Customers also have different expectations of how a social enterprise controls expenses and invests profits than they do of a private limited company, as customers expect to see evidence of how profits, often made through volunteer work and donations, are invested to fulfil a social need.

When you are comparing two concepts, you need to think about what the concepts have in common (similarities) and how they are different. Your answer does not need to be evenly balanced with an equal number of similarities and differences. Sometimes, it may feel like you are pointing out the obvious; for example, in this response pointing out that both business types have high operating costs. However, noting this relatively straightforward similarity then opens the response to a more complex explanation of how the costs might be different, as well as a distinction in the expectation of customers about how the profits are directed, which improves the overall quality of the response. This strategy can be applied any time you are responding to a question with the task word 'compare'.

**Mark breakdown:**
- 2 marks for similarities
- 2 marks for differences

**Top tip**
You do not need to have an equal number of similarities and differences to gain full marks. One similarity and three differences, or three similarities and one difference, will also be sufficient for full marks.

**c**  Beautiful Blooms may have the objective to fulfil a market need, which means that Beautiful Blooms would be focusing on meeting specific expectations of customers (e.g. online ordering or free delivery) or providing a product or products that may not be available in the market (e.g. plants or gifts).

Alternative answers may include to increase market share, but you can't use 'to meet shareholder expectations' as this business is a sole trader.

**Mark breakdown:**
- 1 mark to identify an objective listed in the Study Design other than to make a profit
- 1 mark to describe the objective and link it to Beautiful Blooms

**d**  Decision-making involves responding to a situation, challenge or issue through identifying and assessing the options available and selecting the most appropriate action from the range of alternatives. The owner of Beautiful Blooms first needs to identify the objective and criteria to be achieved; in this case, to have the most appropriate business structure for the current and predicted level of profit. Then they will need to identify the options: to stay as a sole trader or change to a private limited company. To analyse the options, they will need to assess the strengths and weaknesses of each business type relating to profit; for example, consideration of cost and complexity and whether profits will be high enough to justify a significant increase in the cost of administering a private limited company when compared to the minimal cost for a sole trader. From there, the owner can select the best alternative and implement it.

To gain full marks for this response, you need to refer back to the stimulus material, where it is pointed out that a significant increase in profit is the catalyst for needing to decide whether to remain a sole trader or change to a private limited company structure. Reading the paper in its entirety and planning how you will incorporate the stimulus into your responses are useful strategies to apply during reading time.

**Mark breakdown:**
- 1 mark for explaining the concept of decision-making
- 1 mark for explaining how Beautiful Blooms may apply a decision-making process
- 1 mark for making explicit reference to choosing between sole trader and private limited company based on the given objective of making a profit

**Top tip**
Students need to do more than explain decision-making to achieve full marks for this question. A clear link needs to be made between how decision-making is used when considering the appropriate type of business structure for a business such as Beautiful Blooms.

**e** The manager of Beautiful Blooms is responsible for running the business and making decisions that will increase profitability and success. The suppliers sell resources (like raw materials such as flowers) and equipment that will be used by Beautiful Blooms in its production process. For managers, it is in their interests to select reliable suppliers that will deliver resources within the required timeframe and at the lowest possible cost, in order to maximise profits. Meanwhile, suppliers expect to be paid in a timely manner, and it is in their interests to ensure their products are of high quality and are reliable to get repeat business.

A conflict of interest may arise relating to the cost of supplying and delivering high-quality products, within a required timeframe. Like the manager of Beautiful Blooms, suppliers would also be seeking to increase the profits in their own businesses. Higher quality products usually have higher production costs, and a fast delivery service can also be more costly, therefore making resources more expensive for Beautiful Blooms to purchase from suppliers. The manager of Beautiful Blooms would be seeking to minimise costs in order to maximise profit; however, to increase sales, they need to ensure they are sourcing high-quality resources. For suppliers, they would be losing profits if they were to drop their prices too low; however, for the manager of Beautiful Blooms, if a supplier's prices are too high they may choose to buy resources from an alternative supplier.

> To work out how the interests of the manager and suppliers of Beautiful Blooms may be in conflict, you first need to identify and outline the interests of each stakeholder. From there, you can draw out the implications of these interests and the potential points of conflict between stakeholder interests. Using paragraphs is a useful strategy to order your thinking and writing: the first paragraph outlines the interests of each stakeholder and the second paragraph examines the relevant interests and potential points of conflicts arising from those interests.
>
> **Mark breakdown:**
> * 1 mark for outlining the interests of managers
> * 1 mark for outlining the interests of suppliers
> * 2 marks for demonstrating the contrast between these interests and the potential for conflict

**Question 3**

**a** A business that aims to improve effectiveness is typically focused on improving quality and the degree to which stated objectives are met. By closing three of the seven stores, Arrow Sports is able to direct its resources towards meeting increased demand for online shopping through improving the website. The purpose of the closure, and focusing instead on online shopping, is to increase sales. This may also subsequently improve the achievement of objectives such as increased profit and increased market share, thereby improving the effectiveness of operations at Arrow Sports.

> For this question, you need to make the connection between closing stores and reallocating resources as a means of improving business performance, and in turn, improving effectiveness. While a definition of effectiveness is not required, you need to demonstrate an understanding of the concept as part of the response.
>
> **Mark breakdown:**
> * 1 mark for describing the business objective of improving effectiveness
> * 2 marks for linking the improvement of effectiveness to the closure of the stores and focus on online shopping

**b** The consultative style is characterised by the manager maintaining good relationships with employees and seeking input before making decisions.

By seeking input from employees before decisions are made, the manager can gather a greater variety of ideas and suggestions prior to making the decision, which is a strength because it typically results in better decisions. Discussing and refining decisions with a group of people prior to implementation can also improve long-term outcomes, particularly when the decisions being made are high-impact in nature, like the closure of stores and subsequent redundancies.

However, seeking input and engaging in a consultation process during such a complex and high-risk situation like store closures has some weaknesses. Consultation is a time-consuming process and seeking input could lead to staff feeling confused or uncertain about the change, or how they will be impacted personally. It may lead to conflict or resentment between staff, particularly when management will be responsible for making the decisions about who will keep or who will lose their job, which may negatively affect corporate culture in the short and long term.

The consultative style is not the most appropriate style for a high-risk situation involving store closures and widespread loss of jobs. While it may be effective for Gary to source input from a smaller team of trusted people about the implementation process, widespread consultation takes a long time and could result in staff feeling confused or uncertain, which may result in conflict and/or an erosion of culture overall.

> For the evaluation, you need to consider both the strengths and weaknesses of the consultative management style, in the context of store closures. To improve your response, ensure you link the strengths or weaknesses to the characteristics of consultative style, such as how decisions are made or the amount of input sought from employers. To conclude the response, ensure that your overall opinion about the appropriateness of this style is linked back to the key arguments you have made, in order to achieve full marks. While this solution states that the consultative style is not the most appropriate style, a valid argument can also be made in support of the style.
>
> **Mark breakdown:**
> - 2 marks for strengths/benefits of the consultative management style during the change (store closures and/or job losses)
> - 2 marks for weaknesses/limitations of the consultative management style during the change (store closures and/or job losses)
> - 1 mark for an opinion about the overall appropriateness of the consultative style in this context, supported by the relevant points outlined in the strengths and/or weaknesses

c   Gary will need to use planning and leadership skills when closing the three Arrow Sports stores.

Planning involves being able to analyse the situation and determine the most appropriate methods and strategies to achieve specific objectives. In this case, Gary is seeking to close three stores, make a significant portion of the workforce redundant and invest resources into the website and online shopping. In the planning phase, Gary will need to consider whether Arrow Sports is able to maintain high levels of customer service and quality throughout the change period, consider the most appropriate allocation of resources and ensure Arrow Sports achieves long-term success and competitive advantage.

To successfully achieve the desired outcomes for Arrow Sports, it will be essential for Gary to be an effective leader during this period. It is likely that the store closures will be a stressful and uncertain time for many employees; thus Gary can model leadership through being an active listener, demonstrating empathy, addressing concerns quickly, managing conflict when necessary and applying motivation strategies. By being openly committed to the objectives, sharing his vision and influencing people constructively, Gary can lead Arrow Sports through this complex change effectively.

> While this solution outlines planning and leading as management skills Gary will need to use during the store closures, all management skills from the study design can be justified as relevant to this question.
>
> **Mark breakdown:**
> - 2 marks for outlining the characteristics of a relevant management skill (× 2)

# TEST 3: MANAGING EMPLOYEES

## Question 1

A sanction strategy is a negative or punitive consequence, such as demotion, whereby an employee is given a reduced status. Sanctions are best used when a worker is not performing as expected or not adhering to corporate governance rules. By demonstrating their willingness to take action, managers can deter other employees from similar behaviour.

SOLUTIONS – TEST 3

This term has been updated in the 2023 Study Design to include the word 'strategy'. The response above includes detail about what the term means and then, in order to gain the second mark, provides extra information about when and why it might be used.

**Mark breakdown:**
- 1 mark for giving correct characteristic(s) of a sanction strategy
- 1 mark for detail or appropriate example

## Question 2

A motivation strategy likely to have a positive impact is career advancement in the form of promotion. The intrinsic motivation resulting from a promotion (making a worker proud of their achievements and status) has the potential to motivate for a longer period than an extrinsic and short-term tactic, such as a rise in pay.

This response states a type of strategy and then illustrates how it might motivate in the long term. The strategy is an intrinsic tactic, with the worker empowered and willing to do more or better in their new raised status.

**Mark breakdown:**
- 1 mark for stating a motivation strategy listed in the Study Design

**Top tip**

Workers can be motivated by many things other than just the obvious monetary compensation and external benefits. Although intrinsic rewards are more challenging for a business to engineer or facilitate, especially in large organisations, they are well worth the thoughtful consideration and effort required, as workers are then much more likely to stay motivated in the long term. Managers must first take the time and make the effort to get to know their workforce in order to be aware of what is important to them and what are their key motivators.

## Question 3

The human resource manager assists in setting long-term business goals and then puts into place appropriate strategies to source and manage the workers, who then work to meet the set objectives. The human resource department works to recruit, select and retain staff with the right skills to achieve objectives, such as to make a profit. Workers are vital to an organisation because without the right employees, the work cannot get done and no business objectives will be achieved.

This response essentially repeats the two points to be made for a high-scoring answer, so that's not really required; however, emphasising each point adds a little extra business language and demonstrates breadth of business knowledge to ensure this answer is awarded the second mark.

**Mark breakdown:**
- 1 mark for showing how human resource management works to set and/or achieve business objectives
- 1 mark for added detail or a second valid point

**Top tip**

It is common to be asked to explain how human resources or operations effectively achieve business objectives as this is covered in both Unit 3 Area of Study 2 and Unit 3 Area of Study 3. In the exam, this is generally as part of a multipart question that may also require definition of terminology, identification of concepts, demonstration of relationships between concepts and/or suggestions of suitable strategies. The key skill with multi-part questions is to read carefully and ensure you respond to all parts.

## Question 4

a  Lawrence and Nohria's Four Drive Theory says that organisations are somewhat shaped by human nature, as workers are influenced by different biological motivations that managers must find out to be able to effectively motivate individual employees. The drives are: the drive to acquire and achieve, referring to pay, incentives and status; the drive to bond and belong, associated with social connection; the drive to challenge and comprehend, in reference to workers learning and not being bored by simple work; and the drive to define and defend, especially with regard to doing work they consider to be valuable. All drives occur at the same time, with different emphasis in different people, and the aim is to find balance through continual task adjustment. Job duties and responsibilities can be designed and expanded to best motivate individual employees in all four drive areas; however, in reality the potential for a job to appeal to all drives, without any over-emphasis, is difficult to achieve.

> The answer covers the main components of the theory without going into too much detail, as it is not a high mark allocation. This particular question does not ask for how a manager might use the theory. Reading time will show that the next question covers this, so there is no need to do so here.
>
> **Mark breakdown:**
> - 1 mark for providing characteristic(s) of each of the four components of the theory (× 4)

**b**  A manager might apply Lawrence and Nohria's theory to motivate workers who are driven by bonding and belonging through on-the-job mentoring programs, collaborative team tasks, using two-way decentralised management styles and holding social gatherings. These strategies add to employees' sense of being a valued part of a bigger entity and provide opportunities to build supportive work relationships that increase feelings of belonging, enhancing job satisfaction.

> This response offers various strategies to implement this aspect of the theory. Only one way was required, so there is no need to cover all four key theory elements. The important thing is to ensure your answer clearly links back to the theory itself.
>
>    Watch out for normal English use of words in questions. In this case, 'apply' is not used as a task word, so there is no need to respond by analysing anything. If you are unsure due to the nerves of examination reading time, simply check the marks; an analysis question would be allocated more than the two marks allocated here.
>
> **Mark breakdown:**
> - 1 mark for showing how the theory might be applied
> - 1 mark for added detail or showing understanding of practical business implementation or consequences

**c**  Both Lawrence and Nohria's and Locke and Latham's theories provide a framework for managers to guide their assessment of worker needs and structure their planning to meet these needs. They both refer to the need to challenge workers and require managers to know their workforce well in order to work out what drives them, what goals they can commit to or the needs they have already satisfied. Differences between the theories include that Lawrence and Nohria say workers are influenced by internal biological needs, all four of their drives at the same time but with different emphases that can change over time, while Locke and Latham focus on external goal-setting to motivate employees to be productive and rely more on the achievement of that goal before moving on to the next. So Locke and Latham focus on achieving one fixed goal at a time, while Lawrence and Nohria aim for constant adjustment across all fours drives to ensure a job has the potential to offer all four areas of motivation.

> As this question is allocated four marks, you can work out that you have to give two similarities and two differences between the theories. These can be mixed together, as long as they are clear to an assessor. However, you cannot number, list or bullet point your answer, because the task word is 'compare' and so this question must be answered in paragraph form.
>
> **Mark breakdown:**
> - 1 mark for giving a similarity between the theories (× 2)
> - 1 mark for giving a difference between the theories (× 2)

## Question 5

**a**  On-the-job training refers to strategies such as experienced staff mentoring new employees, learning while completing the work with close supervision and support, or professional development provided as part of the workday. Off-the-job training indicates workers are learning at a training provider such as a TAFE or business school, perhaps doing online self-paced competency-based learning at home, or shadowing a worker at another workplace to learn their similar systems and duties. Differences include that on-the-job training involves learning while completing regular work tasks and is most often done at the regular workplace, while off-the-job training has a dedicated focus and is done away from the regular workplace.

This answer very methodically defines each term and then specifically states the difference between them. You don't have to structure your response in this way, but following a pattern every time you answer the same kind of question can ensure you automatically revert to that pattern in the exam, helping you to not miss any expectations for the particular task word.

**Mark breakdown:**
- 1 mark for giving characteristics of each type of training (× 2)
- 1 mark for showing the difference between the two concepts

> **Top tip**
>
> When there are opposing concepts like on-the-job and off-the-job training, you might easily mix them up under the stress of exam conditions. It's a good idea to spend some time working out memory cues for opposing terms and to leave time at the end of tests to go back and check you have not switched definitions. A reminder for these terms could be something like on-the-job = on-site and off-the-job = off-site or off work.

**b** Allocating financial resources for existing staff to mentor new employees allows for a positive induction, but redeploys the staff member away from their usual duties, causing a drop in the rate of productivity. This takes money away from core business, and once an employee has trained they may leave, benefiting a competitor. However, poorly inducted or mentored workers make more errors that require rework, can cause safety risks to themselves and others, are unable to offer competent customer service and are less confident in their work and so less productive. Therefore, training employees is very much worth the financial investment.

This response could also have included that a well-inducted worker is more likely to stay at the business, and in general a well-trained workforce is safer, more confident and capable, more loyal and the business benefits from being able to reallocate multiskilled workers. It could have been mentioned that the mentor may benefit from the arrangement in terms of feeling valued as an expert, or refining their skills through teaching others. It is important to focus on on-the-job training. You could state the benefit(s) of training using their workplace equipment, or the disadvantage(s) of using this equipment for training rather than for more productive work by a skilled staff member. However, the answer above already has enough detail to be awarded full marks.

**Mark breakdown:**
- 1 mark for illustrating the various costs associated with a type of on-the-job training
- 1 mark for giving an argument for why the cost is worth it to the business, or the consequences of not training

## Question 6

**a** The seminar and golf day to develop better teamwork at Corporate Electrical is an example of off-the-job-training because it was held away from the workplace and employees were not completing their regular work duties.

As it is specifically called for in the question, it is important to mention the case study. However, if you are completing a case study section with sub-questions (indicated by a, b, c and so on), you should always refer to the stimulus material. If there is a business or manager name, use it in your response; however, that alone is not enough because any business name could be substituted. You must link some aspect of the business situation to the Study Design concepts to show your understanding of the practical application of theory.

**Mark breakdown:**
- 1 mark for giving the correct type of training with relevant reference to Corporate Electrical

**b** One advantage of off-the-job training, such as the off-site seminar for Corporate Electrical, is that workers can focus fully on the training rather than having to worry about also completing their regular duties while learning something new. A second advantage is that external experts can be hired to provide best-practice, cutting-edge training that may not be part of the skillset of existing employees, and can demonstrate using equipment and performing activities that may not be available or possible at the worksite.

When you are asked for two things, it is a good idea to practise responding methodically by starting sentences in a similar way to those in the answer or using words like 'first' and 'second'. Following this pattern will ensure you are less likely to forget to do the second required task. This response could also have mentioned allowing the organisation to go on with everyday business activities while workers train, ensuring training is done by qualified experts, allowing senior staff to get on with core business rather than being required to mentor, or taking workers out of the work environment to set up a more effective learning environment.

**Mark breakdown:**
- 1 mark for providing an appropriate advantage of the specified type of training (× 2)

c   To improve short-term employee motivation, Anthony may motivate lower managers by using the strategy of performance-related pay. Monetary bonuses related to improved work performance are useful to set motivating targets and can improve the rate of productivity for that set project, or designated period of time, until the bonus has been awarded. If employees are interested in monetary rewards, they will increase their efforts to achieve the target and thus gain the increased pay. The business benefits by being able to increase productivity at key times or for important projects. However, being goal focused and extrinsic, a one-off payment is not a long-term motivator and so, although it may initially prevent Corporate Electrical staff from looking elsewhere for higher remuneration or challenge, will only be effective until the specified target has been met.

Alternative answers could include career advancement or support strategies; however, they must be linked to the case study scenario, with likely impact shown. It is important to note that this question focuses on short-term motivation.

**Mark breakdown:**
- 1 mark for suggesting a short-term motivation strategy
- 1 mark for providing a reason why this is an appropriate suggestion for Corporate Electrical
- 1 mark for giving further reason(s) and/or business impacts

d   Maslow's Hierarchy of Needs claims that five categories of needs influence an individual's behaviour, as they strive to fulfil each level and move up to the next. The first level is physiological needs, where the business pays employees satisfactory wages in order to afford day-to-day essentials like food and shelter. If those needs are not catered for, a worker cannot focus on anything else until they are met. The next level is safety, referring to personal security, stable employment and health. After that, love and belonging become important, including building social connections at work. Next is esteem, whereby employees look for recognition of their efforts, respect and empowerment. The final level is self-actualisation, when workers are looking to fulfil their full potential, perhaps through professional development or sabbaticals.

To reduce staff turnover, Anthony could apply the principles of Maslow's theory at Corporate Electrical by getting to know which stage of the hierarchy his lower managers are at then providing opportunities for those supervisors to strive for the next level of need. Some supervisors still at the lowest level may be motivated by higher remuneration, others who are moving to the esteem level might want to be mentored to improve career prospects, and those at the highest level may be looking for more challenge to improve job satisfaction. By providing what each manager needs, Anthony can keep his workers motivated and retain them for longer, thus reducing staff turnover.

Be careful to note the number of marks when you are describing theory as you can go too far in providing detail, wasting both test time and writing space. As a rough guide, if the page is A4 and your writing is of average size, around two to three response lines per mark should suffice.

Explaining a concept involves detailing the cause and effect (i.e. 'this thing is this way because it has this consequence'). By providing what workers need, this manager can reduce staff turnover as workers are motivated to stay at the business. It is important to refer to the question to show you are staying on track.

For further detail on this past examination question, see the *2018 VCE Business Management examination report* on the VCAA website.

**Mark breakdown:**
- 2 marks for giving key characteristics of the theory
- 2 marks for detailing how the theory could be used at Corporate Electrical and in relation to staff turnover

# TEST 4: MANAGING EMPLOYEES

## Question 1

Performance management aims to improve overall business performance by aligning the evaluation of individual performance with business objectives. A business can use different strategies to assess the degree to which each individual employee contributes to the achievement of business objectives. Performance management can be used to inform decisions about promotion for employees who are exceeding expectations, or the need for corrective action for employees who are not meeting expectations.

> For full marks, your definition needs to be expanded to include at least two points to describe the meaning of performance management. In the solution, the first sentence is typical of what you would read in a glossary and the second and third sentences expand on how performance management aligns individual performance with business objectives.
>
> **Mark breakdown:**
> - 1 mark for the link between individual performance and achievement of business objectives
> - 1 mark for expanding to reference performance management strategies or how performance management can be used by a business

## Question 2

Management by objectives is a performance management process whereby goals of individual employees are agreed to by the employee and management, and individual goals are aligned with the overall business objectives.

Management by objectives ensures that the goals and efforts of each employee are directed towards the achievement of overall business objectives. By aligning individual goals with business objectives, employees and managers have an understanding of employee responsibilities, strategies to improve productivity and clarity regarding the role of each employee to achieve business objectives.

For the employee, management by objectives is an empowering performance management strategy as they are involved in setting goals and determining how these goals will be achieved. Employees can incorporate personal objectives into management by objectives, allowing for them to highlight areas of need such as training or identify additional responsibilities to take on, which may lead to career development opportunities or promotion.

> While a definition is not required as part of the answer, it is important that you clarify the meaning of the strategy as part of your explanation. In the solution, this is done as a description at the beginning of the answer, and that description is referred to in relation to both the achievement of business objectives and employee objectives.
>
> **Mark breakdown:**
> - 2 marks for showing how management by objectives achieves business objectives
> - 2 marks for showing how management by objectives achieves personal objectives

## Question 3

Appraisal is a performance management strategy that improves the efficiency of a business. Efficiency measures how well a business is using resources, including labour, to achieve business objectives. Appraisal is a formal assessment of employee performance against a predetermined set of criteria over a period of time. Because appraisal is a strategy whereby the criteria is predetermined, criteria can be tailored towards measuring the efficiency of employees. Through the process, employees can receive positive feedback about their performance and constructive feedback about areas for improvement, and training needs can be identified.

> All performance management strategies from the Study Design can be proposed for this question; however, when selecting your strategy, it is important to make a logical link between the employees as a labour resource and how the strategy you propose can help a business to improve efficiency.
>
> **Mark breakdown:**
> - 1 mark for identifying an appropriate performance management strategy
> - 2 marks for providing valid reasons why the strategy will improve efficiency of a business

## Question 4

**a** In a workplace like V-Steel, where there is an agreement to determine pay and conditions, employees are responsible for fulfilling their responsibilities and adhering to working conditions, allowing the business to achieve its objectives. When it comes time to negotiate the new agreement, V-Steel's 230 employees need to be engaged in the process. This may include voting on approval of an agreement or consulting with their union as part of collective bargaining.

The Fair Work Commission is the national workplace tribunal responsible for setting minimum wages and employment conditions. For a workplace such as V-Steel, the Fair Work Commission is responsible for approving the new agreement negotiated between employees and employers, as well as ensuring it meets the 'better off overall test' when compared with the industry award and that all parties comply with the agreement. The Fair Work Commission may also be involved in regulating industrial action during the agreement negotiation period, facilitating workplace disputes or addressing unfair dismissal claims.

> In this response, you need to tailor the role of each participant to the stimulus material provided; in particular, the use of an agreement to determine pay and conditions. Providing a generic response may lead you to include unrelated information (such as the Fair Work Commission being responsible for creating awards), which may result in the response being allocated less than full marks.
>
> **Mark breakdown:**
> - 2 marks for detailing the role of employees in the workplace
> - 2 marks for detailing the role of the Fair Work Commission

**b** One strength of using an agreement is that employees and the business can tailor wages and conditions to suit the context of the business, meet employee expectations and support the achievement of business objectives. Another strength of using an agreement is that wages and conditions of an agreement will exceed the minimum wages and conditions set out in the relevant industry award. Building in higher pay and improved working conditions may attract higher quality employees to the business and, in turn, improve overall business performance. However, a weakness of this is that it can be more expensive to implement the pay and conditions outlined in an agreement when compared to the award, leaving the business more vulnerable to reduced performance if it can't attract high-performing employees.

Another weakness of using an agreement is that it is a very time-consuming process for the employer and employees to undergo the negotiation and approval process, sometimes resulting in conflict within the workplace or even industrial action. This can have a negative impact on the achievement of business objectives during the negotiation period.

> When planning your response, draw on the logical reasoning as to why a business would or would not choose to implement an agreement over an award. Consider how an agreement can be tailored to improve overall business outcomes, including the achievement of business objectives and the positive aspects for employees, as well as the potential drawbacks.
>
> **Mark breakdown:**
> - 1 mark for providing and briefly explaining a relevant strength of using an agreement (× 2)
> - 1 mark for providing and briefly explaining a relevant weakness of using an agreement (× 2)

**c** A similarity between awards and agreements is that they need to cover the matters set out by the 11 National Employment Standards, such as maximum weekly hours of work, leave entitlements and working arrangements. However, an award uses the National Employment Standards to establish the minimum wages and conditions for an industry, whereas an agreement is negotiated at the enterprise level and must exceed the safety net of minimum wages and conditions as established by the award.

Another similarity between awards and agreements is that they both require the involvement of the Fair Work Commission. However, the role of the Fair Work Commission differs for each. The Fair Work Commission is responsible for creating and reviewing all modern awards, but rather than creating content, the Fair Work Commission is responsible for examining the details of agreements and approving them.

SOLUTIONS – TEST 4

Awards and agreements can be a challenging part of the course, so being able to recognise how they are similar and different can be a complex skill to demonstrate. In the solution provided, each of the similarities are linked to core aspects of workplace relations in Australia: the 11 National Employment Standards and the involvement of the Fair Work Commission. Regardless of whether a business is using an award or agreement, the National Employment Standards need to be met and the Fair Work Commission will be involved, so these are logical similarities to include. To achieve full marks, the structure of the solution allows for how the standards are met and how the Fair Work Commission is involved to frame the topic sentence for each paragraph as the similarities, with the rest of the paragraph dedicated to describing how they differ.

**Mark breakdown:**
- 2 marks for similarities between awards and agreements
- 2 marks for differences between awards and agreements

**d** Mediation is a dispute resolution process that could be used to resolve the dispute between Miya and the management of V-Steel. A strength of mediation is the involvement of a neutral and objective third party to facilitate discussion between the two parties to work towards the resolution of the dispute. This mediator is not responsible for offering suggestions or solutions. Rather, they are there to help parties to resolve the dispute about safety practices themselves, which can empower both parties to work together and may minimise the negative impact that workplace dispute can have on culture or business performance.

A drawback of mediation is that the mediator may not have an in-depth understanding of the safety practices in place at V-Steel, which may hinder the process. In addition, either party can withdraw from mediation at any time, leaving the dispute unresolved. Another disadvantage of mediation is that the resolution is not legally binding.

Overall, mediation is an appropriate method of dispute resolution for V-Steel, allowing Miya and V-Steel management to work together proactively to address the safety concerns and resolve the issue with the shared objective of making workplace safety a priority.

Arbitration is an acceptable response to this question; however, it is a less common method for resolving disputes and will result in a legally binding decision. There would need to be assumptions and statements made about the dispute being more serious in nature in order for a response involving arbitration to be awarded full marks.

**Mark breakdown:**
- 2 marks for detailing the strengths of mediation as a method to resolve the dispute between Miya and V-Steel management
- 2 marks for detailing the weaknesses of mediation as a method to resolve the dispute between Miya and V-Steel management
- 1 mark for drawing a logical conclusion about whether mediation is an appropriate method to resolve this dispute

**Question 5**

Dismissal and redundancy are both forms of termination. Dismissal occurs when a business terminates employment due to unacceptable behaviour or conduct of an employee. Redundancy also results in the business terminating employment; however, instead of being linked to poor or unacceptable behaviour, redundancy occurs when the person's job is no longer necessary, typically because of management decisions like a restructure, closure, technological change or merger. Dismissal is an involuntary form of termination, whereas redundancy may be either voluntary or involuntary termination, depending on the circumstances.

An exit interview or counselling may be conducted in the case of both dismissal and redundancy, as part of the transition out of the workplace. For employees who are made redundant, the employer may go above and beyond legal requirements by using outplacement services to provide additional support for employees as they prepare to transition into a new job. This may include assistance with resumes, preparing for job interviews or career counselling. In contrast, dismissed employees would not typically be offered outplacement services, as the nature of dismissal does not require the business to support the employee to find a new job.

This question can be broken down into three parts: 1. distinguish between the termination methods; 2. distinguish between the entitlement considerations for each method; and 3. distinguish between the transition considerations for each method.

**Mark breakdown**
- 1 mark for providing the characteristic(s) of dismissal
- 1 mark for providing the characteristic(s) of redundancy
- 1 mark for clearly showing the difference between the two terms, including a reference to entitlement considerations
- 1 mark for clearly showing the difference between the two terms, including a reference to transition considerations

# TEST 5: OPERATIONS MANAGEMENT

## Question 1

The successful management of operations is a key contributor to overall achievement of business objectives at Chef@Home. Operations is responsible for maximising the efficiency and effectiveness of the production process at Chef@Home, including sourcing inputs, introducing technologies, managing materials, improving quality and minimising waste. The elimination of waste is an objective of Chef@Home that is ultimately achieved through decisions and strategies implemented by the operations management team, such as selecting recyclable boxes, bags and containers, investing in an automated production line and sourcing raw food ingredients from local suppliers.

When planning this kind of response, consider the role of operations and the different strategies an operations manager can implement to improve business objectives, such as minimising waste. From there, consider which aspects of your generic understanding of this concept can be written to suit Chef@Home and the stimulus material provided.

**Mark breakdown:**
- 2 marks for outlining the relationship between operations and business objectives
- 1 mark for referencing an objective of Chef@Home and linking that objective to operations management

## Question 2

The three key elements of the operations system are inputs, processes and outputs.

Inputs are resources that are used in the production process of a business. For Chef@Home, inputs include raw ingredients, packaging, capital equipment (such as that used for the automated production line, computers and other machinery), labour resources, recipes and time. Chef@Home owns some inputs, such as equipment, and sources others, like raw ingredients and packaging, from local suppliers. In future, it may source these from overseas suppliers.

Processes involve the transformation of inputs (resources) into outputs (cook-at-home meal kits). For Chef@Home, processes may include developing and refining recipes, taking box orders, assembling containers, portioning ingredients, assembling ingredients into boxes, keeping all ingredients cool and distributing the completed boxes as per customer orders. Chef@Home utilises an automated production line to prepare and package ingredients.

Outputs might also be applied in the answer; however, keep in mind that outputs (in this case, the meal boxes) can be the more challenging element to provide expanded detail about in the response, given the production of only one type of product in this scenario.

**Mark breakdown:**
- 1 mark to identify the three elements of the operations system: inputs, processes, outputs
- 2 marks to relate one operations element to Chef@Home
- 2 marks to relate a second operations element to Chef@Home

## Question 3

Forecasting involves using past and present data to analyse trends and predict future events. The purpose of forecasting is for the business to be able to plan production and anticipate future sales to minimise uncertainty.

Forecasting can be used to improve efficiency, as it is predicting the future requirements for resources in order to meet customer demand and achieve business objectives. It can help Chef@Home to anticipate demand, which is important for a business that utilises perishable raw materials, and ensure an adequate level of materials are on hand to avoid overproduction waste.

By using forecasting, Chef@Home may be able to anticipate future demand more accurately and minimise the need for sourcing from overseas suppliers, thus addressing the risk of underproduction and improving effectiveness. Not being able to meet customer demand may result in a loss of sales or an increase in customer complaints, which would impact Chef@Home's ability to meet business objectives related to profit and market share.

Chef@Home's current supply issues increase the complexity of using forecasting and may lead to unplanned overproduction or underproduction if the estimates are incorrect. Therefore, if Chef@Home implements forecasting, it is necessary for it to regularly analyse data and communicate effectively with suppliers, in order to minimise negative impacts on efficiency and effectiveness.

> To be able to analyse how forecasting can be used to improve efficiency and effectiveness, you will need to demonstrate an understanding of the strategy, which may include reference to the limitations of forecasting as a strategy. Then you need to draw out the relationship between forecasting and efficiency, and forecasting and effectiveness, as separate concepts. Examples of how efficiency may be linked to forecasting include minimising waste of perishable ingredients or avoiding overproduction. Examples of how effectiveness may be linked to forecasting include meeting customer demand or purchasing from local suppliers.
>
> For further detail on this past examination question, see the *2020 VCE Business Management examination report* on the VCAA website.
>
> **Mark breakdown:**
> - 2 marks for explaining the relationship between predicting trends and anticipating the resources required to meet demand; this may include reference to the limitations of forecasting as a strategy
> - 1 mark for linking forecasting to efficiency
> - 1 mark for linking forecasting to effectiveness

## Question 4

Recycling is the process of converting materials that would otherwise be thrown out as waste into new objects or materials. Chef@Home uses 'recycle' as a strategy to reduce waste, leading to minimising its carbon footprint by prioritising the use of recycled inputs through sourcing recycled boxes, bags and containers for use in production. In addition, if Chef@Home promotes its use of recycled materials, this may improve its reputation and increase sales, which can improve profit.

While using recycled inputs is more environmentally friendly, a limitation of using recycled inputs in operations is that it can be more costly to purchase recycled materials, which increases production costs and may decrease profit.

> This question is tricky because the case study does not include detail about implementing the 'recycle' strategy to minimise waste in production, but rather through the sourcing of recycled inputs.
>
> **Mark breakdown:**
> - 1 mark for describing the strategy of 'recycle'
> - 2 marks for indicating the interrelationship between the recycle strategy and minimising waste at Chef@Home

## Question 5

Chef@Home is committed to reducing its carbon footprint and uses a variety of strategies that demonstrate its focus on reducing environmental impact by going above and beyond legal requirements. This has influenced management decisions about the minimisation of waste in production and the use of recycled packing, including boxes, bags and containers, even though the business is not legally required to do so.

Another way that corporate social responsibility considerations can influence decisions made by management is in relation to where the business sources inputs. Chef@Home has a policy to source all inputs from local suppliers, which minimises the distance travelled for delivery and subsequently reduces the environmental footprint. In addition, this decision has a positive impact on the economy of the local community by supporting other local businesses. Having this policy in place will influence decisions made about sourcing inputs from overseas suppliers in future, including considering ethical and environmental impacts.

Two logical aspects of corporate social responsibility related to Chef@Home are social considerations (local suppliers) and environmental considerations (minimising carbon footprint). However, you can include references to other corporate social responsibility considerations in your response, even though they may not be mentioned in the stimulus, based on appropriate assumptions around future decisions that may be made by management.

**Mark breakdown:**
- 2 marks for detailing a relevant corporate social responsibility consideration related to decision-making at Chef@Home
- 2 marks for detailing a second relevant corporate social responsibility consideration related to decision-making at Chef@Home

## Question 6

An automated production line is a process that is controlled by a computer and consists of equipment and machinery organised in a sequence, with the purpose of adding parts to goods as they proceed through each stage of the production line. For Chef@Home, this can improve efficiency of operations because it can increase output, reduce the cost of production and improve productivity. However, the equipment required for an automated production line is an expensive investment for Chef@Home to make and will require costly regular maintenance to ensure it functions well. When an automated production line breaks down, it can negatively impact productivity and efficiency.

Using an automated production line also improves standardisation and can enhance precision and accuracy, which in turn minimises waste. This would be important given the need to provide the correct amount of ingredients for each meal and Chef@Home's broader objective to reduce its carbon footprint. However, it can require ongoing training of employees to correctly use and monitor the machinery, which can be costly and time-consuming, leading to a temporary reduction in efficiency of operations.

Overall, for Chef@Home, an automated production line is an appropriate strategy to improve the efficiency of operations because it increases the accuracy and precision of production, leading to the standardised provision of ingredients for customers to make meals at home. It will also minimise waste, which links to one of the main objectives of Chef@Home: to reduce its carbon footprint.

Your evaluation needs to weigh up both the strengths/benefits/advantages and weaknesses/limitations/disadvantages of the automated production line and provide an overall opinion about the appropriateness of this strategy; however, to gain full marks, the key ideas need to be related to improving efficiency at Chef@Home.

**Mark breakdown:**
- 2 marks for the strengths of an automated production line for Chef@Home to improve efficiency of operations
- 2 marks for the weaknesses of an automated production line for Chef@Home to improve efficiency of operations
- 1 mark for an opinion about whether it is an appropriate strategy for Chef@Home

**Question 7**

A benefit of sourcing from overseas suppliers is that they may be able to reliably source and deliver ingredients and other inputs that are not available locally or that are difficult to source from local suppliers. This could lead to Chef@Home being able to source a greater variety of ingredients to offer a wider range of meal boxes for customers and create a competitive advantage.

However, sourcing from overseas suppliers would breach Chef@Home's current policy to source from local suppliers, which may negatively impact business reputation and lead to a decrease in competitiveness and lower market share. Another limitation is that there may be disruptions to delivery from overseas that may be difficult to forecast or anticipate, which could significantly impact its ability to source all the ingredients required for the meal boxes. Without having strong relationships with local suppliers, Chef@Home may find it difficult to consistently meet customer demand in a timely manner.

Another benefit of sourcing ingredients from overseas suppliers is that due to different workplace conditions, the ingredients may be less expensive than sourcing from local suppliers. This can decrease costs, which may increase profits and allow Chef@Home to invest more in the business by purchasing more equipment or expanding the business. However, a weakness of sourcing perishable food items from overseas is the increased risk of wastage, as travelling long distances can mean food spoils or is less fresh. Increased wastage or decreased quality may negatively impact profits, either through an increase in expenses or a decrease in sales.

This question is assessing the key knowledge dot point relating to global considerations, specifically whether the business should source from overseas suppliers. What makes this question challenging is that your focus needs to be on the strengths and weaknesses of multiple considerations, as opposed to describing or explaining the considerations, as per question 5 (relating to corporate social responsibility considerations). Careful reading of the question and planning of the response may be something you could do in reading time when faced with a complex question like this.

For further detail on this past examination question, see the *2020 VCE Business Management examination report* on the VCAA website.

**Mark breakdown (global marking):**
- 1–2 marks for a limited discussion of the considerations relating to sourcing ingredients from overseas, or only a generic explanation of one or two considerations without weighing up the strengths and weaknesses relating to the consideration
- 3–4 marks for a thoughtful discussion of some considerations related to sourcing ingredients from overseas, with some attention paid to both the strengths and weaknesses of the considerations
- 5–6 marks for a detailed and sophisticated discussion of multiple considerations related to sourcing ingredients from overseas

**Top tip**

When questions are marked globally, you need to consider the component parts of the response as well as the answer as a whole. The final mark will be influenced by the level of detail that is included, as well as the overall coherence of the response. Questions are typically marked globally when there is a higher mark allocation (generally 4 to 5 marks and above) and there is no specified number of key points or ideas that can be 'counted' in the response.

# TEST 6: OPERATIONS MANAGEMENT

## Question 1

Quality control is a reactive strategy, as it refers to a process of checking or inspecting products and rejecting defects as waste or items to recycle into the production system. This process may occur at any stage in production, but most especially before final products are shipped to customers to ensure only the highest quality goods are distributed. ChocYum Pty Ltd could implement this strategy by having quality inspectors testing chocolate products after manufacturing, but before they are packaged to save further wasted effort or resources. Inspectors may look for visual defects in the chocolate (such as misshapen products, discolouration or bloom) and they may conduct fragrance or taste tests to check for intended standard outcomes across batches. Quality control is important for ChocYum Pty Ltd as it prides itself on manufacturing the finest-quality products and any defects could negatively impact sales through damaging its brand and business reputation.

This response gives detail on the characteristics and process of quality control, and then goes on to illustrate how the case study business might implement the strategy and why. It is key here to show you can derive from case study materials the appropriate processes and outcomes for the specified type of business. You don't need to know exactly how chocolate is made or tested, but you do have to show you can make an educated guess as to appropriate points, drawing on business operations theory from concepts covered by the Study Design.

**Mark breakdown:**
- 2 marks for stating correct characteristics of quality control
- 1 mark for providing an appropriate strategy
- 1 mark for a clear link to ChocYum Pty Ltd

### Question 2

*The following is an actual student response taken from the 2019 examiners' report.*

The first stage of operations relate to inputs, these are the resources used to create an end output. For a manufacturing business like ChocYum Pty Ltd inputs are vital including cocoa and sugar but most importantly staff to run and operate the machines. Similarly, to a service such as a haircut human resources are an essential part of operations that are required to create the end output. However, they differ in the processes stage which relates to transforming inputs to outputs as often a manufacturing business is able to automate production using machines though a service business like haircuts can't do this. Finally, the other key difference is in outputs which relates to the end product, a manufacturing business like ChocYum Pty Ltd create a tangible output that can be stored. Unlike a service businesses like a haircut who can't store a haircut and it is intangible.

Source: *VCAA 2019 VCE Business Management examination report*

Appropriate similarities include comparison of common system elements and the fact that both kinds of business oversee an operations system in general. Differences include whether items are more likely to be standardised or customised and whether a customer needs to be present or not during production. There were no marks allocated for referring to the case study; however, you can demonstrate you understand the kind of business the case study is by mentioning it, when appropriate, in your response.

For further detail on this past examination question, see the *2019 VCE Business Management examination report* on the VCAA website.

**Mark breakdown:**
- 2 marks for providing suitable manufacturing and service operations system elements to show similarities
- 2 marks for providing suitable manufacturing and service operations system elements to show differences

### Question 3

ChocYum Pty Ltd could use artificial intelligence (AI) to ensure high-quality chocolate product outputs. The computing power of AI can be used to monitor and regulate the production process; for example, in adjusting the temperature of facilities and machines to ensure inputs are kept at optimum temperatures. AI is able to learn over time; for example, at ChocYum Pty Ltd to adjust settings to manage the many external variables such as weather, the heating up of working machinery and even an unexpected event such as a power failure. AI could also monitor the quality and standardisation of the products by adjusting input amounts and types to ensure best results in the mix, removing defective products to maximise standardisation and communicating with specialist machines to perfectly time the entire production process of these perishable products.

Appropriate suggestions could include robotics, computer-aided design, computer-aided manufacturing and online services. It is important to note the directive to NOT discuss automated production lines. Watch out for exclusionary or negative question components.

**Mark breakdown:**
- 1 mark for giving an appropriate technological development strategy
- 2 marks for giving detail about the strategy and how it might be used to improve production at ChocYum Pty Ltd

SOLUTIONS – TEST 6

## Question 4

One strategy to improve the efficiency of materials management at ChocYum Pty Ltd would be Just in Time (JIT). JIT involves determining when resources are needed and only having them delivered or onsite when the production process actually requires the resource. ChocYum Pty Ltd may use a JIT approach when ordering inputs, like perishable ingredients such as milk. This improves efficiency by cutting refrigerated storage requirements, saving space and energy, and avoiding waste through spoilage.

> An option is given here to discuss efficiency OR effectiveness, meaning you don't need to cover both. Alternative answers might include master production schedule or materials requirement planning.
>
> **Mark breakdown:**
> - 1 mark for suggesting an appropriate materials management strategy
> - 1 mark for added detail or linking to ChocYum Pty Ltd

## Question 5

Reusing inputs helps an organisation make the most of its resources and saves costs associated with waste such as storage, removal and disposal. ChocYum Pty Ltd could improve efficiency through reusing resources, such as returning defective or misshapen chocolate products back into the earlier stages of the production line. As long as the ingredients are the same and there are no adverse health and safety aspects, chocolate defects may be melted down and remade into correctly shaped products for sale. This allows reuse of ingredients and so improves the efficiency of resource use through waste minimisation.

> This response makes assumptions about the case study that are not in the stimulus, but that can be assumed through the type of product being made. Even if they are actually handmade chocolates, the above answer still rings true. In reality, ChocYum Pty Ltd may not be interested in reusing fresh ingredients due to a reduction in output quality, but that doesn't matter for the purposes of a 'suggest' question. You are allowed to give your opinion, as long as it appears to suit the case study and you give sensible reasons for your proposition.
>
> **Mark breakdown:**
> - 2 marks for giving reasons why the 'reuse' strategy suits ChocYum Pty Ltd
> - 1 mark for linking to improving efficiency at ChocYum Pty Ltd

## Question 6

*The following is an actual student response taken from the 2019 examiners' report.*

Lean management is the process of maximising customer value whilst reducing the amount of waste created by the business operations system. It includes four key principles such as pull, takt, one-piece flow and zero defects. ChocYum Pty Ltd can use pull to increase their efficiency as this is where customer demand pulls goods/services through the operations system. This means that the production of chocolate at ChocYum will be directly linked to production which can help reduce overproduction of chocolate thus reducing the amount of ingredients wasted leading to the more efficient use of resources, improving ChocYum's operation system's efficiency. Takt is the speed a product needs to be produced at to meet customer demand. This can help ChocYum ensure that there is always enough chocolate being produced to meet customer demand as this helps create a continuous flow of chocolate production which can lead to more customers being satisfied by ChocYum as there is enough chocolate being produced to meet the demand, that's improving the effectiveness of ChocYum's operation system. Zero defects will also help reduce the amount of wasted chocolate and resources as ChocYum will aim to produce chocolate with no errors/defects, thus improving the use of ingredients at ChocYum's operations system, improving effectiveness.

Source: *VCAA 2019 VCE Business Management examination report*

The student answer needs to be extensive and would be awarded the full six marks. It describes lean management, including the key principles, initially specifies efficiency, and then goes on to detail how focusing on a pull system, takt and zero defects would suit and be implemented in operations for this case study. Alternative answers could describe one-piece flow.

For further detail on this past examination question, see the *2019 VCE Business Management examination report* on the VCAA website.

**Mark breakdown (global marking):**
- 1–2 marks for description of some lean management key principles
- 3–4 marks for all key principle descriptions and brief benefit(s) for business in general or ChocYum Pty Ltd
- 5–6 marks for detailed key descriptions linked to ChocYum Pty Ltd and appropriate potential benefits in relation to efficiency or effectiveness

**Top tip**

Acronyms can help you remember a series of concepts such as those needed for lean management. Many students use the acronym 'POTZ' to remember pull, one-piece flow, takt and zero defects. You may be able to make up something that has more meaning for you. It is something worth thinking about early and then practising throughout the year, so when it comes to the examination you can then just write the acronym as soon as writing time starts to recall the key concepts with ease.

### Question 7

ChocYum Pty Ltd opening a United-Kingdom-based facility will allow for product manufacturing to be geographically closer to some of the customer base. This would mean less refrigerated transport required and shorter lead times to get the product to the retailer and ultimately to the final customer. A weakness of manufacturing so far away would be that the expected high quality may be difficult to supervise and control. Facilities may not follow the set policies, processes and systems to meet their corporate culture or equipment specifications, perhaps allowing substandard products to be distributed and consequently negatively impacting the brand. As part of ChocYum's vision is to provide 'products of the finest quality', the owner may weigh up the costs and benefits and decide overseas manufacture may well be cheaper and faster, but is not worth possibly damaging the business reputation through inferior products, and so may choose to retain control of the entire supply chain to ensure standardised high-quality end products.

This response provides a strength that is related to the case study business type, but is also fairly general in nature, although made more specific by mentioning refrigeration. The weakness refers to product quality, which again could be a general point to be made about any business. However, this answer quotes part of the vision from the initial stimulus to provide a clear and close link to ChocYum Pty Ltd.

**Mark breakdown:**
- 1 mark for providing an appropriate strength
- 1 mark for providing an appropriate weakness
- 1 mark for drawing on stated strengths and weakness to conclude
- 1 mark for added detail or close links to ChocYum Pty Ltd

**Top tip**

It is important to note that operations management allocates and coordinates resources towards the most efficient and effective achievement of business objectives. No business objectives can be achieved without operations as this is the area in charge of the production of the actual good or service and the starting point for all other business activities. Without operations, finance has nothing to cost and marketing has nothing to market. The reliance of a business on operations management makes it particularly important to carefully consider the capabilities of a supplier if outsourcing this area of management responsibility.

### Question 8

Corporate social responsibility refers to a business going beyond legal requirements in order to demonstrate consideration for people, including staff, customers and community, as well as the place where it operates. One environmental sustainability consideration might be to ensure that all packaging is low-carbon, recyclable or biodegradable. There would be a lot of packaging of inputs that ChocYum Pty Ltd does not control, but it may make choices based on whether suppliers use low-emission packaging, such as paper. After all, ChocYum Pty Ltd has to deal with storage and removal of inputs waste as well as its own from its production process, such as excess packaging trimmings, so being able to recycle would lower costs. Although it is not legally required and most chocolate products come wrapped in foil for freshness, this business may also commit to using mostly low-carbon or already recycled paper in its own external packaging. This would allow ChocYum Pty Ltd to 'climate label' its products as having environmentally sustainable wrapping, appealing to customers with environmentally conscious social attitudes.

> This answer begins with a definition that is not strictly required, but does help focus the response. Note the use of 'people' and 'place/planet' (profit is missing here) to refer to the triple-bottom-line accounting often associated with corporate social responsibility considerations.
>
> **Mark breakdown:**
> - 1 mark for selecting a relevant corporate social responsibility consideration for the ChocYum Pty Ltd operations system
> - 1 mark for demonstrating the relevance of the consideration
> - 2 marks for linking the corporate social responsibility consideration to environmental sustainability

**Top tip**

Examination questions generally ask you to optimise an operations facility in some way through suggesting and justifying strategies, so you need to be able to apply the theory to the given case study situation. As ever, it is not enough to simply mention the name of a stimulus business; specific details must be included to demonstrate understanding. If any other business name can be inserted and your answer still makes sense, then the link will not be awarded any marks.

# TEST 7: UNIT 3

### Question 1

a   Business objectives are the aims, goals or targets of the business. They are the reason for operating and what all human resources are working towards. Common business objectives listed in the Study Design include to make a profit, increase market share, improve efficiency, improve effectiveness, fulfil a market need, fulfil a social need or meet shareholder expectations.

> **Mark breakdown:**
> - 1 mark for providing characteristics of the term
> - 1 mark for relevant detail

b   Resignation refers to when an employee makes a choice to end a work relationship and leave an organisation. Depending on the terms of the work contract, written notice is usually required to give the employer time to organise the outgoing worker's entitlements, as well as the transition of a new worker into the position to ensure work continues.

> **Mark breakdown:**
> - 1 mark for providing characteristics of the term
> - 1 mark for detail or relevant example(s)

c   Quality assurance is a proactive form of quality management that involves high-quality inputs going into the production system to ensure high-quality outputs and to minimise defect waste. In Australia, businesses can demonstrate their quality assurance status by advertising compliance with quality management standards set by the International Standards Organisation (ISO 9001).

> **Mark breakdown:**
> - 1 mark for providing characteristics of the term
> - 1 mark for detail or relevant example(s)

# Area of Study 1

## CASE STUDY

**Question 2**

**a**  DanceNow is a public listed company, as the stimulus states it is 'listed' and has 'shareholders', meaning shares are being sold to the public. Businesses may 'float', or sell shares, to raise capital for expansion or to meet other objectives. Public companies have an unlimited number of shareholders and shares can be freely traded on the stock exchange, without the need for owner approval. A public listed company is often indicated by having 'Limited' or 'Ltd' as part of the company name and uses a highly complex business structure, with a high degree of accountability and compliance legally required. A real-life example of a public company is the Coca-Cola Company, in which the international public can buy shares across various stock exchanges.

> Alternative characteristics include that it is incorporated or that owners have limited liability. This response takes evidence from the case study and includes various related business terms to demonstrate a breadth of understanding. As it is worth three marks, the answer includes detail that is not specifically asked for, such as why businesses may sell shares, adding richness to the description. Similarly, giving a correct real-life well-known example that the assessor is sure to recognise shows you know the subject.
>
> **Mark breakdown:**
> - 1 mark for identifying the correct type of business
> - 2 marks for providing correct characteristics of public companies

**b**  Stakeholders have a vested interest in the business, meaning they have a personal reason to care about business success. Stakeholders include groups such as owners and managers who want to meet business objectives, employees who want to keep their jobs, customers who want the product or service, competitors who can be impacted by the success or failure of others and the general community where the business operates and who may be concerned with the environmental impact of operations.

Shareholders are part business owners who have invested their money to get a return when the business makes a profit or when the value of their shares increases. Shareholders have voting rights according to how many shares they own, and so can have some impact on company decisions.

DanceNow would have many different types of stakeholders, including the uniform suppliers, whose own businesses may be impacted by the success of DanceNow. As part owners, DanceNow shareholders are also key stakeholders. However, not every stakeholder is a shareholder; there are many different types of stakeholder groups and each has a unique vested interest.

> The task word 'distinguish' requires some explanation of each term and then clear differentiation. Stakeholders versus shareholders is a common question, because many students get confused, or at least write responses in a confused way. Make sure you can articulate the relationship. Keeping to three separate paragraphs can help you methodically cover all three points required. There is no stated requirement in this question to refer to the case study; however, when a question is included as part of case study questions, it is always a good idea to incorporate some information from the stimulus.
>
> **Mark breakdown:**
> - 1 mark for providing characteristic(s) of stakeholders
> - 1 mark for providing characteristic(s) of shareholders
> - 1 mark for clearly showing the difference between the two terms

**c** Corporate culture can be 'official', in that it is published in business policies and communications, or it can be 'real' in that it is indicated by the everyday behaviours of the employees. At DanceNow, managers are content and seem compliant when Hester disseminates information; however, it turns out that the managers are not actually capable and serious negative impacts result. Therefore, the real corporate culture is to agree with Hester and commit to undertaking the set tasks, but then to go away and not complete the tasks, or fail to forecast and act on future issues, such as the reducing enrolments, or the consequences of transport delays.

You may also see 'real' corporate culture noted in places as 'unofficial'; however, 'real' is the Study Design term. This question has specifically asked you to use the case study information in your answer, so make sure your links to DanceNow are crystal clear, meaning no other business name could be substituted because you have given information that is only applicable to DanceNow.

**Mark breakdown:**
• 2 marks for demonstrating real corporate culture at DanceNow using information from the stimulus

**d** Hester uses a persuasive management style. We can tell this because she is informative and clearly communicates management decisions, giving reasoning and potential impacts on staff.

This management style is appropriate to some extent; Hester's middle managers are content in their work, as demonstrated by them staying in their jobs, and they feel Hester is giving them lots of information and transparent decisions, which is good for motivation and staff retention. However, although this persuasive management style is working to keep employees satisfied, managers are actually not capable of some required tasks, so this style is not appropriate to futureproof the business. Managers are not forecasting or developing and implementing action plans in relation to external concerns, such as dropping enrolments and supply issues due to transport problems.

A more direct management style may be more suitable when working with newly appointed workers like in this situation, such as the stricter authoritative style, whereby Hester would simply direct the managers as to what they need to do without providing them with reasons. This style may act to better motivate managers, through them being more comfortable with Hester taking responsibility for areas in which they are not competent. This would improve the rate of productivity by avoiding the situation reaching crisis levels, as Hester would remain in control of decision-making and be able to make directives about best-practice actions to take, and so could ensure the work is done effectively and the rate of productivity improves as crises are avoided, while her workers gain experience.

To respond to the specific question, this analysis needs to show how the style being used is working and not working, demonstrating the degree to which the style is appropriate in this particular situation. There are benefits with some positive outcomes; however, there are also clear problems and so a different style has been suggested and linked with the likely outcome. Analysis requires you to discuss elements and show how they impact on or make up the whole, in this case how the management style is working and impacts of using that style on the business. An alternative relevant answer that could be presented would be for a more consultative style, empowering and upskilling middle managers to be more responsive.

**Mark breakdown (global marking):**
- 1 mark for correctly identifying Hester's management style, with suggestion about appropriateness
- 2–3 marks for explanation of correct management style with reference to DanceNow to show appropriateness
- 4 marks for in-depth analysis with close links to DanceNow, including reference to the extent of management style suitability for this business scenario

**e** Hester demonstrates the management skill of communication because she transmits messages clearly; she advises her employees of decisions and background reasoning, evidenced by the fact that they feel content and well informed. Communication also involves listening, and the stimulus hints that Hester may listen to her workers by stating that she is approachable.

Communication is the management skill most clearly implied by the stimulus material. Leadership, decision-making or interpersonal skills might be appropriate, but you would have to use information from the case study to show exactly why you are suggesting those skills instead. Delegation and planning are clearly not suitable suggestions for the presented situation. The question is not asking for a definition, but you will still need to show you understand the skill.

**Mark breakdown:**
- 1 mark for providing an appropriate management skill
- 1 mark for closely linking the stated skill to DanceNow

**f** The business scenario at DanceNow indicates that employees are satisfied with communication from the CEO because they are stable and content. However, the newly appointed middle managers are not capable of getting on with all required tasks without further direction, in particular forecasting and developing and implementing action plans to prepare for future issues. Although she is currently setting managers tasks, they are not doing them or showing initiative; therefore, Hester must improve in selecting the right person, with the right skills, for the right job, at the right time. This shows that Hester needs to better develop the management skill of delegation.

Delegating involves Hester retaining responsibility, and this would suit the situation well, as her managers are inexperienced and so require more supervision, such as reporting back to their CEO periodically on developing plans or meeting targets. Better delegation skills would improve business effectiveness as Hester could be sure she has passed down tasks to competent managers with the skills to get the job done. This would mean crises would be avoided, such as by having a new enrolment stream or finding local suppliers, thus improving the overall rate of productivity.

'Assess' is a higher order task word that therefore attracts higher marks. It requires you to use various pieces of information from the stimulus (text or chart) to show you understand the business situation, what is and isn't working and how things could be improved. In this particular case, you must make a link with effectiveness to gain full marks.

**Mark breakdown (global marking):**
- 1 mark for suggesting a management skill with some use of the case study
- 2–3 marks for suggesting a suitable management skill, making relevant links to DanceNow
- 4 marks for discussing various aspects of case study information to suggest a suitable management skill to develop, making close links between the particular situation, the need for the suggested skill and management effectiveness

# Area of Study 2
## STRUCTURED QUESTIONS

### Question 3

Maslow's Hierarchy of Needs says that five categories of needs influence an individual's behaviour as they strive to fulfil each level and move up to the next. The first level is physiological needs, where the business pays employees satisfactory wages to afford day-to-day essentials, like food and shelter. If those needs are not catered for, a worker cannot focus on anything else until they are met. The next level is safety, referring to personal security, stable employment and health. After that, love and belonging become important, including building social connections at work. Next is esteem, whereby employees look for recognition of their efforts, respect and empowerment. The final level is self-actualisation, when workers are looking to fulfil their full potential, perhaps through professional development or sabbaticals. A manager must build relationships with workers to know them well enough to be able to offer them the next level of need, so they are motivated to perform.

> This question is asking for the 'key elements'. In Test 3 for Unit 3 Area of Study 2 , question 6d asked for a 'brief description'. The response is an expansion of the response to question 6d. It has essential elements that would satisfy either question, but with a little more detail here on how a manager might apply the theory (to gain the full four marks).
>
> **Mark breakdown (global marking):**
> - 1 mark for providing some theoretical detail
> - 2–3 marks for providing at least three key elements of the theory, as well as demonstrating some theoretical understanding
> - 4 marks for providing all key elements of the theory, as well as demonstrating clear theoretical understanding

### Question 4

Locke and Latham's Goal Setting Theory relies on effective goal setting to motivate employees to be productive with targets, generally agreed on during annual performance reviews or at target-setting conferences. There are five aspects to consider when setting effective goals: clarity, challenge, acceptance, feedback and complexity. A manager might set time-bound productivity targets that are clearly communicated, mutually committed to and agreed on, and appropriately challenging and complex to stretch the worker's skill set and avoid boredom. Scheduling regular opportunities to give timely feedback and acknowledge progress or accomplishments will further motivate the worker to higher performance levels.

So to motivate an underperforming employee in practice, a supervisor might co-create a monthly target with an employee that provides an appropriate challenge to extend their skills, but not overwhelm them. Feedback through a short conference can be given after a fortnight to make any adjustments needed, such as further support, training or refining of goals, and then the manager can provide positive reinforcement when the target has been met. This structured process will motivate the worker towards better performance, work confidence and job satisfaction, because they have been empowered to co-create goals and then given feedback, support and appreciation.

> More detail could be added here to clearly describe the five goal considerations; however, with only two or so marks devoted to theory description, it would be a wasted effort to provide more than four to six lines of response. The additional task here, for another four to six lines, is to apply the theory to improve the given scenario.
>
> It can be a little confusing, especially due to nerves during reading time, but this is another reminder to watch out for the normal English use of words in questions. In this case, the word 'apply' is again not used as a discrete task word requiring you to apply something, but refers to you linking appropriately to a given business scenario where a manager might apply something. The way you need to answer is very similar; however, for full marks you must remember to 'demonstrate' your contention by using relevant reasoning as evidence of why your suggestions are useful.

## Question 5

An appraisal is a performance management strategy that involves a conference between a manager and a worker where both parties are expecting and understand the process, and have had time to prepare. Usually conducted annually, it is a regular opportunity for a manager to give positive and constructive feedback on a worker's performance based on collected evidence, to set future goals and to ask for worker feedback. Appraisals contribute to achieving business objectives because required business targets can be set, potential barriers discussed and plans made to provide the worker with the support they need to get the work done, while maintaining a high rate of productivity. Employee objectives can also be aided by appraisal, in that it is an appropriate time to raise concerns or areas of need such as organising work-related training towards future personal goals (e.g. promotion).

This response sets out what an appraisal is and then gives suggestions as to how appraisals aid in the achievement of business objectives, and then employee objectives, using an example to demonstrate understanding. Another relevant example here might be to discuss future employment goals of the employee, to ensure business objectives are met in the area of future labour-force planning. Alternative responses could include detailed descriptions of self-evaluation or employee observation.

**Mark breakdown:**
- 1 mark for providing the characteristics of a performance management strategy other than management by objectives
- 1 mark for describing how that strategy can achieve business objectives
- 1 mark for describing how that strategy can achieve employee objectives

## Question 6

Unions act on behalf of workers, or groups of workers, to negotiate above-award work conditions, entitlements and benefits. They provide free legal advice to members about workplace rights and responsibilities. Unions also monitor and hold employers to account for their workplace responsibilities, including worker safety, and this may mean representing employees at the Fair Work Commission. Unions may cause conflict by organising and mobilising groups of workers to act in support of fellow workers or for better workplace conditions. This might mean advising work-to-rule actions, where workers only do exactly what is in their job description and no more, or even strikes, whereby production ceases until demands are met. Workers themselves may be intimidated by the more powerful and vocal union groups, and Australian union memberships have decreased since the 1990s. However, workers who are union members enjoy the expert support and sense of safety in numbers that union membership and representation brings.

This question requires you to read the question very carefully to note and respond specifically to the set focus on unions only.

**Mark breakdown (global marking):**
- 1–2 marks for either positive or negative aspects of the role of unions
- 3 marks for both positive and negative aspects of the role of unions in the workplace
- 4 marks for detailing both positive and negative aspects of the role of unions in the workplace, demonstrating clear understanding

## Question 7

Retirement is a method of terminating a workplace arrangement. It can be instigated by the worker when they choose to end their participation in the workforce, or can be triggered by a person's age, according to Australian law. A person who has reached retirement age is considered to have fulfilled their duty to work as an active member of society, and they can then access part or full pension as part of government-subsidised welfare (depending on their assets and ongoing earnings from other work).

Employers may benefit from specialised voluntary early retirement packages, before workers reach retirement age, to cater for business objectives or targets. These may include reducing their workforce or invigorating their labour force with younger workers, who may be more creative, energetic or committed or more recently trained in contemporary best practice. However, age-based and early retirement can drain the business of expert workers and leave a knowledge gap, with new employees taking some time before being as productive. Overall, early and planned age-based retirement can be a predictable way to reinvigorate an organisation's workforce, but the associated loss of expert knowledge and skills must be considered in future workforce planning to ensure ongoing workforce stability and productivity.

This response needs to be focused on the impacts of retirement for the employer only. If it was from the worker's perspective, more could be said about receiving lump sum payments without necessarily being banned from rejoining the workforce, or perhaps the issue of workers not wanting to retire due to not having personal interests to occupy them, or enough savings to fund their desired lifestyle, or because they want to keep contributing and feeling valued at work. However, these points are not relevant for the question. This question provides another lesson in the need to read carefully during reading time, to break up the question to highlight the important tasks as soon as writing time begins, and to plan your response before you launch into writing your answer.

**Mark breakdown:**
- 1 mark for providing positive characteristic(s) of retirement
- 1 mark for providing negative characteristic(s) of retirement
- 1 mark for concluding based on points made about the suitability of retirement for terminating workplace arrangements from the employer's perspective

# Area of Study 3

## STRUCTURED QUESTIONS AND SHORT STIMULUS

## Question 8

Computer-aided design is a technological development strategy involving computers being used in the product design process. For example, based on collected data, a computer may make modifications to mechanical parts, such as those used in cars, and then run simulated tests to determine the best option to meet the goal set. This design process is much more resource efficient than manual parts design and testing, as there is no need to make and install a modified part and then crash-test real cars for every design alteration. Without human intervention, the computer can make multiple and precise part modifications to gain the best result under all kinds of varied situations, minimising the use of physical resources for making part alternatives or for real-life prototype tests.

Alternative responses include describing the use of automated production lines, robotics, computer-aided manufacturing techniques, artificial intelligence and online services. In Test 5 question 9, you were asked to 'evaluate the use of an automated production line as a strategy to improve efficiency'; that response required strengths, weaknesses and a conclusion. However, the question here only asks for an 'outline', so a brief explanation of a relevant development is all that is required for full marks. Once again though, as is common when considering operations management, the focus is on efficiency.

**Mark breakdown:**
- 1 mark for providing a relevant technological development strategy
- 1 mark for linking the suggested strategy with improving the efficiency of operations management

## Question 9

Operations management is the business function that uses resources, including labour, to get the actual work of the organisation done. Business objectives are the goals and targets set by the organisation to be achieved, which would include making a profit so the business stays viable. Business objectives cannot be met without the outputs of goods and services produced from inputs by the operations system. For example, profit cannot be made if the core work done in business operations has not produced anything to sell, or if operations processes have been inefficient by producing too few or too costly products. Meeting business objectives is dependent on efficient and effective operations management.

You cannot get full marks just by defining the given terms, although this will get you some marks as showing understanding is important. You need to make it clear how these concepts work together in a business scenario.

**Mark breakdown:**
- 1 mark for showing understanding of the terms
- 2 marks for providing detail on the cause-and-effect relationship between the concepts

## Question 10

Total Quality Management involves all workers taking personal responsibility for continuous improvement across all processes within the operations system. Data is collected to ensure decision-making is based on facts. A manager could use this strategy by implementing a system of customer feedback, such as a customer survey. Consulting customers ensures that the business is producing what customers want to purchase, of the right quality and at the right price. Survey feedback goes back into the operations system as an input to improve processes, and results in producing more saleable products and services. This then improves effectiveness, as the operations system is better able to meet business objectives, such as fulfilling a market need, increasing market share or making a profit.

Read this question carefully to note that the focus is now on effectiveness, not efficiency, so you need to mention achievement of business goals and objectives.

**Mark breakdown:**
- 1 mark for suggesting a suitable strategy related to Total Quality Management
- 2 marks for giving reasons or examples of how the suggested strategy would improve effectiveness of operations

## Question 11

'Reduce' is a waste minimisation strategy that refers to decreasing the amount of production hard waste that has to be removed and taken for incineration or disposal, such as to a landfill, as well as minimising the volume of pollutant emission by-products. 'Reduce' also means having less going into the production process so there is less waste generated as an operations output. The efficiency of the operations system can be improved by using the strategy of 'reduce', as less resources are used as inputs, so less waste is created along the production process, resulting in higher efficiency. The strategy of 'reduce' can also improve effectiveness because business objectives can be better achieved by reducing waste, such as by meeting targets in relation to lowering waste production. Corporate social responsibility objectives focused on the environment, like achieving cleaner production processes that generate lower associated emission outputs, can also be achieved.

This response gives various characteristics of the stipulated strategy and then links specific 'reduce' tactics with improved business outcomes. Both efficiency and effectiveness are considered. No other waste minimisation strategies should be mentioned here as only 'reduce' is stipulated. All parts of the question must be addressed to gain full marks.

**Mark breakdown (global marking):**
- 1–2 marks for providing characteristics of the 'reduce' strategy with some links to operations
- 3 marks for linking characteristics of the 'reduce' strategy to either efficiency or effectiveness of operations
- 4 marks for linking characteristics or outcomes of the 'reduce' strategy to both efficiency and effectiveness of operations

**Question 12**

A corporate social responsibility consideration for an operations system is the environmental sustainability of inputs. Atlas Dining is a real-life business that considers environmental sustainability when sourcing inputs for its at-home master class ingredients. Atlas Dining prepares globally inspired ingredient boxes and associated videos or recipe instructions for customers to make restaurant-quality meals at home. The business pivoted from being a physical restaurant to an opt-in or weekly subscription service in response to the external challenges presented by COVID-19. Managers source local ingredients where possible, reducing the need for carbon-emitting transport, and use 100% recyclable cardboard boxes and refreezable, non-toxic ice packs. The overall concept appeals to environmentally conscious customers, as all ingredients are carefully measured to eliminate the food waste generally associated with an everyday person's weekly shopping and catering efforts. The initiative has been a huge success and profits have exceeded those of the former physical restaurant.

Competitors are a stakeholder, as they have a vested interest in whether similar businesses succeed and are under some pressure to maintain a competitive advantage if they are to keep or increase their market share. For example, Lite n' Easy is a competitor business that delivers weekly food subscription boxes, targeting customer weight loss and convenience. Lite n' Easy's food provision also avoids food waste, but has been criticised over time for using polystyrene tubs, plastic bags and plastic containers. However, to remain competitive, Lite n' Easy offers to collect and recycle bags and tubs.

It's hard to determine if publicised feedback has had a direct impact, or if the two businesses have impacted each other directly. However, it is clear that the actions of one business can influence another business to make operational changes to become more environmentally sustainable and thus maintain or grow its customer base.

Any relevant real-life business example can be used here, as long as you clearly demonstrate why your suggested business is suitable for your response to the specific question; in this case, in relation to corporate social responsibility considerations in operations management. Your answer to the previous test question may have reminded you of an example from class or one you covered in a past assessment, or perhaps a business that you deal with in your everyday life, maybe even your own workplace. Alternative responses may refer to the amount of waste generated from processes or the production of outputs. As this is a longer response, it can help to break your answer into paragraphs to ensure you address all parts of the question sufficiently.

**Mark breakdown (global marking):**
- 1–2 marks for brief or detailed description of a suitable corporate social responsibility consideration
- 3–4 marks for providing detail about a suitable corporate social responsibility consideration in relation to a relevant stakeholder
- 5–6 marks for providing cause-and-effect impacts of a suitable corporate social responsibility consideration, suggesting an appropriate stakeholder, as well as the likely impact on them

# TEST 8: REVIEWING PERFORMANCE – THE NEED FOR CHANGE

**Question 1**

Business change refers to any modification or transformation to the internal or external environment, typically through implementing a new business behaviour, idea or process, such as introducing new technology or implementing staff training.

It is important that your definition contains at least two distinctive parts, features or characteristics related to the concept. When defining a term like 'business change' for two marks, you can address the broader concept of change to gain the first mark, then tailor your response to how a business changes to gain the second mark.

**Mark breakdown:**
- 1 mark for providing characteristics of the term
- 1 mark for detail or relevant example(s)

## Question 2

Business change is inevitable and businesses can respond to change in a proactive or reactive manner. While both approaches to change can increase competitive advantage, when a business takes a proactive approach, it is initiating change; when it takes a reactive approach, it is responding to change after it has happened.

Both approaches are influenced by conditions in the internal and external environment. However, proactive change is a planned approach, meaning the business is more prepared for altered or anticipated factors from the environment, which may result in less negative impact on productivity, morale, use of resources and the achievement of objectives. Meanwhile, a reactive approach is usually unplanned and is a response to unanticipated pressures from the environment, which may result in short- or long-term impacts to business priorities such as productivity, level of sales or corporate culture.

When you are comparing two concepts, you are explaining what the concepts have in common and how they are different. Just a reminder that your answer does not need to be evenly balanced with an equal number of similarities and differences. In this case, proactive and reactive approaches to change are fundamental differences in the way a business responds to change. However, what they have in common can be drawn from more general knowledge about the concept of change, such as change being influenced by what may occur in the internal or external environment. You may notice in the response that the differences between approaches are prefaced by a generalised similarity in order to provide enough detail for full marks.

**Mark breakdown:**
- 2 marks for similarities
- 2 marks for differences

## Question 3

In a highly competitive market, a business can adopt the lower-cost approach to achieve competitive advantage through reducing overall production costs. For a business that sells products at or below industry average, the lower-cost approach can increase profitability, as the cost per unit will decrease, while the selling price is maintained in order to still attract customers when there is a lot of competition. Costs can be reduced in a number of ways; for instance, by reducing direct or indirect costs, by improving efficiency or through reviewing management decisions in other areas of the business. Reviewing decisions may assist the business to maintain market share and competitiveness if competitors are not able to match reductions in costs or price. Further, cost savings and profit can be directed towards setting the business apart from its competitors through the development of new products or innovation.

However, if the reduction in production costs affects customer perception or experience of quality, this can result in a decrease in sales and consequently, negatively impact profitability and competitive advantage. Further, the business may be vulnerable to decline in overall performance if conditions in the external environment change, such as competitors also adopting a lower-cost approach, or a significant increase in direct costs that cannot be entirely mitigated through changing suppliers, such as from a global increase in the price of raw materials.

Overall, in a highly competitive market, a lower-cost approach is most appropriate when a business charges around industry-average prices but is able to reduce production costs and respond to changes in the external environment more effectively than its competitors.

For an evaluation, you need to consider both the strengths and weaknesses of the lower-cost approach in a highly competitive market. To improve your response, ensure you link the strengths or weaknesses to business performance when operating in a market that is highly competitive. To conclude the response, ensure that your overall opinion about the appropriateness of this approach is linked back to the key arguments you have made in order to achieve full marks.

**Mark breakdown:**
- 2 marks for strengths/benefits of the lower-cost approach
- 2 marks for weaknesses/limitations of the lower-cost approach
- 1 mark for an opinion about the overall appropriateness of the lower-cost approach in the context of a highly competitive market, supported by relevant points outlined in the strengths and/or weaknesses

> **Top tip**
>
> In this kind of question, you need to adapt the generic strengths and weaknesses to the specific strategies and circumstances mentioned in the question. In this particular case, you need to link a lower-cost approach to a highly competitive market. This can be done through linking strengths and weaknesses back to increasing sales, increasing profitability, responding to changes in the external environment or outperforming competitors.

## Question 4

**a**  Productivity measures the level of outputs (goods and services) produced by the number of inputs (resources). The rate of productivity growth at Wilkinson's Window Tinting measures the change in productivity levels from year to year. From Year 1 to Year 2, the rate of productivity growth has increased from 2% to 8%, indicating that the purchase of new machinery and automation of the tinting process has improved the rate of productivity through more efficient use of resources. Improved performance in the rate of productivity growth could indicate that Wilkinson's Window Tinting is either utilising the new technology to produce more outputs from the same level of inputs or using less inputs to produce the same level of outputs in an improving capacity.

> While the question does not ask for a definition of productivity or rate of productivity growth, in order to describe how the indicator can be used to analyse performance, you need to clarify what the indicator is measuring and how it is used to determine whether business performance has improved or declined. In the case of Wilkinson's Window Tinting, rate of productivity growth can be used to measure the impact that the investment in new technologies and automation of the tinting process (inputs) has had on the production of outputs.
>
> **Mark breakdown:**
> - 1 mark for outlining 'rate of productivity growth'
> - 1 mark for identifying the improvement in rate of productivity growth at Wilkinson's Window Tinting
> - 1 mark for detailing how the change from Year 1 to Year 2 indicates an improvement in performance

> **Top tip**
>
> In this question, the task word is 'describe', not 'analyse'. The key knowledge dot point this question is derived from refers to key performance indicators as sources of data to *analyse* business performance. So, the question is using the term 'analyse' in this context, addressing how rate of productivity growth can be used to analyse the performance, as opposed to performing an analysis of business performance using the data provided to answer the question. To avoid confusion, read every question carefully and watch out for normal English use of words that are also Study Design terms.

**b**  *The following is an actual student response taken from the 2018 examiners' report.*
The new machinery has helped in improving productivity as it has increased by 6% over one year. This means that the resources (such as time to make the tinting) have been used well (less time needed now with the automated process). Thus, it has improved the business's performance in the sense that they are saving time and being more efficient. Another advantage that the introduction of the machinery has brought is the reduction in number of customer complaints. Perhaps the technology (since it's new) has allowed for the quality of the windows to improve which has satisfied Wilkinson's Window Tinting, as the number of customer complaints is now only 28, in contrast to Year 1 where it was 112. Despite these advantages, the key performance indicators for net profit figures shows that the introduction of this technology has been expensive and therefore their profit has drastically decreased by 24 000 dollars. Since net profit refers to the amount left over once expenses (including the introduction of technology) is subtracted from revenue earned, then it means that the technology was highly priced and therefore they have less profit; meaning that currently they will have to examine their expenses as profit is essential to the business's performance. In addition, the rate of staff absenteeism has increased by an average of 8 days per year per staff member meaning that perhaps the introduction of technology has caused the employees to feel no longer valued as they have been previously the ones doing the tinting. Thus, as employees are a valuable asset to a business' performance, then a lack of them throughout the year suggests that they are not performing as well as in Year 1.

*Source: VCAA 2018 VCE Business Management examination report*

To answer this question well, you need to make logical assumptions about possible reasons for changes to the data from Year 1 to Year 2 at Wilkinson's Window Tinting. Logical assumptions may include a reduction in profits associated with the purchase of new equipment (including training), an improvement in quality (which would lead to a reduction in customer complaints) or automation of the tinting process (which should speed up the tinting process and increase productivity).

For further detail on this past examination question, see the *2018 VCE Business Management examination report* on the VCAA website.

**Mark breakdown (global marking):**
- 1–2 marks for limited detail on the impact the purchase of new machinery has had on key performance indicators; brief description of the trends in the data
- 3–4 marks for adequate detail on the impact the purchase of new machinery has had on key performance indicators; some description of the trends in the data, with reference to some or all of the data
- 5–6 marks for comprehensive detail on the impact the purchase of new machinery has had on key performance indicators, with thorough description of the trends in the data and reference to some or all of the data

**c** After reviewing the performance of the business and identifying the need for improvement, the manager acted as a driving force for change by making decisions and leading change in the operations of Wilkinson's Window Tinting. Problematic areas of performance included the rate of productivity growth and the number of customer complaints, so the manager chose to invest in new machinery and focus on automating the tinting process in an effort to initiate, encourage and foster change, improving achievement of the business objectives. The manager needs to continue to act as a driving force for change by making decisions and being responsive to needs in order to improve other areas of the business, such as controlling costs to improve net profit figures, and better managing human resources to reduce staff absenteeism.

Because this question is asking 'how' the manager is a driving force for change, it is necessary to draw examples from the stimulus material to provide detail on specific actions and decisions the manager has undertaken to initiate and foster change.

**Mark breakdown:**
- 1 mark for describing the concept 'driving force'
- 2 marks for detailing, with examples and links to the data, how this manager has acted as a driving force for change

**Top tip**
There are no definitions provided in the response to this question; rather, understanding of the terms 'manager' and 'driving force' has been woven into the explanation. For instance, in sentence two, key terms relating to the meaning of 'driving force' have been incorporated into the explanation of how the manager has acted as a driving force to achieve business objectives.

**d** The increase in staff absenteeism, from an average of 4 days per year to an average of 12 days per year, indicates that employees are increasingly dissatisfied with their work. Employees can act as a restraining force for change, by resisting or hindering change in a business, when they feel fear or a sense of mistrust about change. By choosing to invest in new machinery and automating the tinting process, the manager of Wilkinson's Window Tinting has fundamentally changed the type of day-to-day work many employees will be undertaking. Perceived threats to job security, established processes, or culture can lead to passive or overt resistance to change. This data reflects a significant decline in employee morale, evidenced by the increase in staff absenteeism. If the workers are absent, the change in work cannot be implemented.

Like the previous question, this question is asking 'how' the employees are a restraining force for change. As indicated by the question, it is necessary to refer to the data directly in your response. To gain full marks you will need to make logical assumptions about the negative impact that new machinery and automation of the tinting process has had on employees.

**Mark breakdown:**
- 1 mark for briefly describing the concept 'restraining force'
- 2 marks for detailing, with examples and links to the data, how the employees have acted as a restraining force

**e** Purchasing new machinery and automating the tinting process are significant and costly decisions for Wilkinson's Window Tinting. By applying the principles of the Force Field Analysis theory, the manager is able to determine the forces that are going to drive or resist change and develop a plan to guide the desired change more effectively.

The first key principle is for the manager to identify and weight the possible impact of the current driving and restraining forces relating to the purchase of new machinery and automation of the tinting process. Examples of driving forces may be enthusiastic managers, pursuit of profit or technology, whereas restraining forces may be reluctant employees, time constraints or organisational inertia.

Ranking is the second principle that entails the manager prioritising the top driving forces to be strengthened and the most dominant restraining forces to be eliminated or minimised. For instance, the manager may identify technology and managers as two driving forces to be strengthened, and employees and organisational inertia as restraining forces to be minimised.

The third principle involves developing an action plan and implementing an appropriate response, with roles and responsibilities allocated for each action. And finally, the last principle is for the manager to evaluate the response, by assessing the degree to which the change has been successful. For Wilkinson's Window Tinting, this may involve reviewing the key performance indicators from before the change and analysing the data to measure any progress made since the change to using new machinery and automating window tinting processes.

When a question asks how a business may apply a theory like Force Field Analysis, it is important that you use a combination of examples from the stimulus material, reasoned assumptions and the theory itself to logically break down how the business will apply each principle of the theory.

**Mark breakdown:**
- 1 mark for detailing how the principle 'weighting' may have been applied at Wilkinson's Window Tinting
- 1 mark for detailing how the principle 'ranking' may have been applied at Wilkinson's Window Tinting
- 1 mark for detailing how the principle 'implementing a response' may have been applied at Wilkinson's Window Tinting
- 1 mark for detailing how the principle 'evaluating' may have been applied at Wilkinson's Window Tinting

# TEST 9: REVIEWING PERFORMANCE – THE NEED FOR CHANGE

## Question 1

A key performance indicator is a source of data that measures business performance. For example, Handy Dandies has collected 2027 data on its percentage of market share and found that it is declining, possibly due to other competitors offering the same or better services. Managers can now use this information to increase business success through planning improvements and resource allocation.

Examples of key performance indicators from the Study Design include percentage of market share, net profit figures, rate of productivity growth, number of sales, rates of staff absenteeism, level of staff turnover, level of wastage, number of customer complaints, number of website hits and number of workplace accidents.

**Mark breakdown:**
- 1 mark for providing the key characteristics of the term 'key performance indicator'
- 1 mark for providing extra detail, linking to Handy Dandies or relevant example(s)

## Question 2

A manager might use net profit figures (income minus costs) to determine the best course of action for this business moving forward. So Handy Dandies' managers may note that net profit figures have increased over the reporting period and feel this is sufficient to keep things the way they are, perhaps also deciding to provide a positive return on investment to the partners. On the other hand, managers may feel other key performance indicator data shows current high net profit figures will not be sustainable without making changes that require decision-making and planning, such as securing more sales by moving to newly settled geographic areas.

This response includes a brief definition of the term and goes on to link to the case study data to clearly demonstrate understanding of the presented business scenario. Other relevant changes may include increasing the labour force to expand services, decreasing production expenses by bulk-purchasing inputs like uniforms, or lowering prices to secure more customers and increase market share. Ensure relevance by linking back to the question through mentioning future decision-making.

**Mark breakdown:**
- 1 mark for providing a general statement about how net profit figures can impact decision-making
- 1 mark for providing detail on how net profit data may be used and/or links to Handy Dandies

## Question 3

According to the graph data, Handy Dandies' percentage of market share has gone down in the reporting period, while the net profit figures have gone up. So, although there has been more income made after costs have been paid, the overall number of transactions in relation to all sales in this market has dropped. These figures show that a relationship cannot be assumed whereby less market share results in less profit. For example, in this case there have been fewer sales, but more overall profit. This indicates that competitors have taken some market share. It does not necessarily mean fewer customers for Handy Dandies, but certainly fewer sales. During the same period, Handy Dandies might have charged more for services since the last report or made production cost savings in operations that have allowed for increased profit. Therefore, in this case, there may be no direct cause-and-effect relationship between the two indicators.

This is a tricky question requiring some complex business thinking. There are close links between the points in this answer and the data provided in the stimulus. Assumptions have been made about what that data might indicate, with contentions backed up by appropriate scenarios. Although connections between indicators can be hypothesised, this response gives reasons why there may be no relationship between the two indicators.
For a VCAA example of this kind of question and expected style of response, see the
*2021 Business Management examination* Part B
(https://www.vcaa.vic.edu.au/Documents/exams/busmngmnt/2021/2021busman-w.pdf)
and associated assessment report
(https://www.vcaa.vic.edu.au/Documents/exams/busmngmnt/2021/2021busmanage-report.pdf).

**Mark breakdown:**
- 1 mark for providing close link(s) to the data provided
- 1 mark for detailing appropriate scenario(s) that may explain the data
- 1 mark for demonstrating understanding of how the two given indicators may or may not affect each other

## Question 4

A reactive approach refers to managers responding to events after they have occurred. For example, after analysing the 2027 data, Handy Dandies may choose to offer new types of in-home services, such as cleaning, in an effort to gain more sales. The sales gain might not necessarily be from an increase in customers, which can attract other associated costs, but from an increase in the number of services Handy Dandies' current customers buy. This services expansion strategy has come about reactively because of an acknowledged data trend, not through forward planning.

This response clearly shows that a reactive approach means making a decision after the fact, by stating this at both the start and end of the answer. To add weight, a detailed example is given that relates well to the given business scenario.

**Mark breakdown:**
- 1 mark for providing key characteristics of reactive management
- 1 mark for providing extra detail, linking to Handy Dandies or relevant example(s)

## Question 5

A proactive management response involves a manager forward-planning before an issue arises. The data shows the rate of productivity growth is increasing, which is positive. Therefore, a proactive management response to this data might be to collect information about the reasons behind this upward trend, then use the results to design new policies to ensure it continues. Policies might involve maintaining the new expected rate of productivity growth by following streamlined processes to support continuously improving practices, such as through training to provide increasingly faster inquiry-to-customer-conversion turnaround times. Setting in place policies before the rate of productivity drops is a proactive approach, as this strategy supports the higher rate of productivity growth while pre-empting a possible issue and acting to minimise the likelihood of that issue occurring.

Being proactive is, of course, the opposite of being reactive. This could have been stated in the response, but it can be better to use your time and space to detail only the term in the question. This response goes into detail to show understanding of the required term and to link closely to the stimulus material by giving appropriate examples. To ensure the mark is awarded, the proposed strategy and required term are linked at the end of the answer, restated in the form of a conclusion.

**Mark breakdown:**
- 1 mark for providing an example of a proactive approach linked to the rate of productivity growth data
- 1 mark for giving a reason why this is an example of a proactive approach
- 1 mark for providing further reason(s), relevant detail or links to Handy Dandies

## Question 6

a   A key performance indicator that Handy Dandies might use to make decisions could be the number of customer complaints. The data indicates that both the market share and the number of sales are decreasing. Perhaps these results are due to decreasing quality of services, whereby customers are making a complaint and then seeking out a competitor for their next nanny or nurse service. An increasing number of customer complaints would indicate to management that decisions need to be made about how to improve service quality. Collected data would be vital here to find out what exactly the complaints are about so that plans could be made to address the particular areas of concern. If an increased number of customer complaints is reported, managers will need to dig deeper into the data to be able to make decisions that improve the specific situation.

A key word in the question here is 'relevant'. Levels of waste and number of workplace accidents do not immediately link to the data provided. Although, if you can show a sensible and close relationship, do so, because there is no specific expected response.
   Other most suitable responses may include:
- rates of staff absenteeism
- level of staff turnover
- number of website hits.

**Mark breakdown:**
- 1 mark for providing a relevant key performance indicator
- 1 mark for demonstrating understanding of how the identified key performance indicator can be used to make decisions
- 1 mark for extra relevant detail or extended close links to Handy Dandies

**b** The number of customer complaints may well trend upwards considering the information given. As the net profit figures are rising, Handy Dandies may be charging more for services. This price rise would naturally increase customer expectations, because they are paying more for nannies and/or nurses than they were before, or than they need to with competitors. The rate of productivity growth is also rising, indicating that Handy Dandies is increasingly able to produce more with less. This may also cause an increase in the number of customer complaints, as employees may be stretched to service more clients, causing a drop in the quality of each service. Or perhaps Handy Dandies has shifted to less-expensive resources, such as equipment that may not perform as well as previously or cheaper uniforms that do not look as smart. The drop in market share and lower number of sales can both be linked to levels of customer satisfaction, as would be demonstrated by the number of customer complaints. If sales are down and market share is going to competitors, it can be assumed that customers are not satisfied and so will make more complaints, trending the number of customer complaints key performance indicator up.

> This response draws extensively on the stimulus data to justify the predicted upward trend in customer complaints, as it links all given indicators to a hypothesised situation. While just referring to one data type would still be correct, it would be difficult to then write enough to ensure you were awarded full marks.
>
> **Mark breakdown:**
> - 1 mark for suggesting a data trend for the key performance indicator identified in question 6a
> - 2 marks for giving reason(s) why this indicator might trend in the suggested way
> - 1 mark for further detail demonstrating a high level of understanding and/or close links to Handy Dandies

## Question 7

After determining driving and restraining forces for change, ranking involves prioritising the forces in order of importance, immediacy or practicality. A manager might use the ranking from Lewin's Force Field Analysis theory to make decisions about what restraining force needs to be addressed first to minimise negative impact. Or the manager may rank the forces in order of how expensive, practical or easy it would be to shift a restraining force to a driving force, such as training employees who may be resisting change due to lack of confidence with new in-home care bookings technology, or incentivising apathetic middle managers with financial bonuses linked to adopting changes aimed at increasing sales. If some things are easiest or cheapest to address, and will make a big impact on the required change, ranking forces will help managers work out which strategies to implement first to encourage a smoother change transition.

> This response shows some understanding of the theory and goes into detail about the particular aspect of ranking. Note that this question does not ask for a definition of the theory, and the low marks should indicate that it is not required; there would not be test time or page space for further explanation. You need to show you understand the theory just by the way you use it in a sentence.
>
> **Mark breakdown:**
> - 1 mark for briefly explaining how Lewin's Force Field Analysis theory might be used
> - 1 mark for demonstrating understanding of 'ranking' in relation to Handy Dandies

## Question 8

Driving forces are those that encourage change transition, such as willing employees, financial opportunities (like government grants) or favourable business environments (like low business-loan costs). Restraining forces are those that hinder business change, such as high operating costs, or resistant managers who don't want to learn new ways of working. One difference between the two concepts is that driving forces support and assist business change, while restraining forces hinder and prevent change. A second difference is that driving forces can result in efficiencies that effectively achieve change goals, while restraining forces are more likely to require action that can add to the costs associated with business change.

In reference to the percentage of market share data, the information shows Handy Dandies is losing a percentage of market share to its competitors. Driving forces to put in place strategies to change this situation might be managers wanting to meet set sales targets linked to their performance evaluations, or low interest rates on business loans to reduce costs. Less-expensive business loans would allow Handy Dandies to invest in new online payments technology that attracts more sales because clients can book and pay for in-home services without needing to call. Restraining forces that prevent strategies to improve percentage of market share figures might be employees not wanting to change how they work or take on new clients, or a competitor in the market attracting Handy Dandies' customers through successful marketing campaigns, convincing customers that they are a more caring alternative for children and elders.

This answer methodically responds to the 'distinguish between' part of the question first and then goes on to link to the case study. You may choose to incorporate both these parts together as you give examples of forces, by making them relevant to the scenario. That approach is valid; however, make sure you include enough points and clear case study links to be awarded the full five marks. As a high number of marks are allocated, this answer provides two examples of each type of force and two differences between the opposing terms.

**Mark breakdown (global marking):**
- 1 mark each for providing definitions or demonstrating understanding of 'driving forces' and 'restraining forces' (× 2)
- 1 mark for clearly showing the difference between the two terms
- 2 marks for closely linking to Handy Dandies, such as providing examples that relate to the specific business scenario

## Question 9

Aside from aiming to be low-cost, Porter's strategy of differentiation involves working to be the business in a market that stands out because of a point of difference or competitive advantage. This could be in relation to the entire business or just a segment; for example, in relation to either of Handy Dandies' nannying or nursing services.

An advantage of using the differentiation strategy would be the potential to improve the number of sales per customer and percentage of market share through offering different or more extensive services than competitors. For example, Handy Dandies might decide to be the only nanny service available that also offers quality home-cooked meals for children. This might encourage customers to book longer nannying hours or further days, increasing sales figures and attracting customers away from competitors that do not offer this service. On the other hand, differentiation can require higher operational costs that drain business financial resources. For this example, costs might include cooking training for employees, further insurance if nannies are to be taking children food shopping, or marketing campaigns to raise awareness of this new offering among both current and potential customers. Managers would need to weigh up the costs and benefits of Porter's differentiation strategic management approach before making decisions about whether to change business systems.

Again, you have not been asked for a definition, but a short outline to demonstrate understanding does not take much time or space and does get your brain into the right space to answer the question. Just know that no marks will be allocated for this part of your response, so minimise the test time you devote to that task. As this is a discussion, no conclusion is required. What is important is that you show business understanding by providing examples that make sense for the scenario given.

**Mark breakdown:**
- 1 mark for at least one advantage of Handy Dandies using the differentiation strategy
- 1 mark for at least one disadvantage of Handy Dandies not using the differentiation strategy
- 2 marks for additional supporting reasons for and against

# TEST 10: IMPLEMENTING CHANGE

## Question 1

Effective business leadership is very important during change. If leadership is ineffective, employees may feel unstable in their positions and productivity will decrease as they worry about losing their job, or spend time looking for new employment. Ineffective leadership may also cause confusion, as change goals and processes may not be clearly communicated, leaving workers without direction. This could cause rework, an increase in defects and duplicate work, because the labour force lacks unity of purpose.

This response starts with a statement that will not attract any marks, but may serve to set you up to write on the topic, getting you ready to deliver clear reasoning. In this particular situation, care must be taken to not switch the terms to respond about effective leadership only, when the question specifically asks about impacts of ineffective leadership. If you are running out of space or time in an assessment, try to stick to providing only what gains marks. Two reasons were provided above about the potential impacts of ineffective leadership during change. Many more alternative impacts could have been given and, as there is no case study, as long as your answer is on-topic, sensible and justified, it will be considered possible.

**Mark breakdown:**
- 1 mark each for providing a relevant business outcome of ineffective leadership (× 2)

**Top tip**
There are various task words that only attract one mark, so we have to be ready for whichever comes our way. Common task/exam/action words include 'state', 'give', 'provide', 'name' and 'identify'.

## Question 2

First, a business might seek new global business opportunities by investigating international options for sourcing raw materials, component parts or other required inputs for operations. Overseas suppliers may be able to supply needed inputs at a cheaper cost per unit than domestic suppliers, often due to lower costs of labour or business regulation, or easier access to raw materials.

A second way to make the most of global opportunities could be to outsource some operations processes to overseas suppliers. Work that does not need to be done physically onsite can now be tendered out globally to skilled workers. This is particularly true of transferable business skills and functions like marketing, research and report-writing.

Other options include overseas manufacture and seeking global innovations. Note here again the suggested methodical formatting of a two-part response to ensure the required two points are made: 'First, this … Second, this …'. To keep you on track and ensure you cover all required parts of the question, you might draft in these sentence starters at the beginning of writing time, before going back later to actually answer the question.

**Mark breakdown:**
- 1 mark for each appropriate way to seek global business opportunities (× 2)
- 1 mark for each reason why the suggested action is suitable (× 2)

## Question 3

Low-risk strategies to overcome employee resistance to change include: clear communication before, during and after the change; employee empowerment through co-creation of goals and sharing of responsibilities; support such as timely access to mentors to answer any questions that arise; and incentives such as bonus payments.

High-risk strategies to overcome employee resistance to change include manipulation, such as only giving employees some information about positive change impacts and no information about adverse impacts, and threat, whereby a manager uses an authoritative style to coerce a worker to make changes or else lose their job.

The difference is that low-risk strategies are more likely to gain employee trust and buy-in for a smooth change transition due to less employee resistance. This generally results in higher staff retention, whereas high-risk strategies are more likely to alienate or distress employees, increasing resistance to change and leading to higher staff turnover.

This response clearly gives a characteristic of each type of strategy and then states the difference between the two concepts for the third allocated mark. As the question stipulates, you must make sure to link your answer to employees and overcoming resistance to change.

**Mark breakdown:**
- 1 mark each for demonstrating understanding of low-risk and high-risk strategies (× 2)
- 1 mark for clearly showing the difference between the terms, linked to overcoming employee resistance to change

## Question 4

Increased investment in technology has the potential to impact managers in a variety of ways. New or innovative technology may cut design or production costs, allowing managers to use resources more efficiently or redeploy finances to other business areas. Innovative technology may reduce production emissions, allowing managers to meet internally or externally set targets. New technology may make complex work easier, improve the safety of dangerous or toxic work, increase the accuracy of precision or repetitive work, remove the need for heavy lifting, or make work faster by allowing for around-the-clock shifts without breaks. All these impacts allow managers to protect workers and use resources more efficiently, including hiring less human labour. Fewer human workers decreases the need for managers to deal with workplace issues, such as monitoring employee break times, providing mandated safety equipment or managing workplace injuries. Training for and using new technology may also change previously habitual workplace behaviours, increasing productivity and allowing managers to maintain closer adherence to set organisational policies and procedures, as well as more readily comply with external regulation, such as changing occupational health and safety or environmental emissions legislation.

As this is an analysis, your response needs to provide enough points to gain the allocated marks. In this case there are four, so you should aim for four relevant points as a minimum. Each point you make needs to be linked back to how it could potentially impact on managers.

**Mark breakdown (global marking):**
- 1–2 marks for demonstrating the relationship between investment in new technology and potential impacts on managers
- 3–4 marks for breaking down four or more aspects of business operations that could benefit from technological solutions and providing associated appropriately aligned positive or negative impacts on managers

## Question 5

a  *The following is an actual student response taken from the 2020 examiners' report.*
Kurt Lewin developed a seminal theory on the best approach a business should take when managing change that involves three main steps, unfreezing the status quo, changing and refreezing. Initially, the manager of Manitta Mining will need to unfreeze the status quo by explaining to its employees reasons for the change, why they need to implement it, who will be affected by it, etc. In this case, Manitta Mining will need to explain the level of workplace accidents that occurred which will explain to the employees why it is essential to adopt the change. During this time, employees may feel scared about the situation and a manager must provide support and openly communicate. Next, the manager at Manitta Mining will aim to apply the change in the second step of the three-step model. In this case, the manager will need to constantly provide feedback and maintain support whilst understanding that staff need to learn to adopt the new operations that have been put in place by the new operations manager. Finally, the business will refreeze and all policies will need to be updated to reflect the change. For example, all new safety procedures would need to be stated in written documents and policies as the change is embedded into their new culture.

*Source: VCAA 2020 VCE Business Management examination report*

This is a high-scoring question, so you are expected to provide a lengthy response. Six marks gives you ample opportunity to cover all aspects of Lewin's Three-step Change Model, as well as link closely to whatever the question indicates. As mentioned before, you cannot just use a business name to get linking marks, but must reference something particular to that case study. In this case, reducing workplace accidents is the current focus at Manitta Mining, but that is not a current concern for every business. You do not need to know for sure that Manitta Mining managers have used this theory, you just have to demonstrate how and why they might put it into practice and the resulting benefits for the business.

For further detail on this past examination question, see the *2020 VCE Business Management examination report* on the VCAA website.

**Mark breakdown (global marking):**
- 1–2 marks for a brief explanation of three stages of Lewin's Three-step Change Model
- 3–4 marks for an explanation of each stage and application of some or all stages of Lewin's Three-step Change Model to Manitta Mining
- 5–6 marks for detailed explanation of each stage and appropriate application of all stages of Lewin's Three-step Change Model to Manitta Mining, with clear links and multiple references to workplace accidents

**b** Manitta Mining may respond to the key performance indicator of 'number of workplace accidents' through increased investment in staff training by running some on-the-job training with experienced or highly skilled staff, demonstrating correct equipment use, or teaching safe materials handling to less-experienced workers. Guiding workers through expected safety controls using their own or similar facility workstations and machinery gives employees a clear idea of what is expected of them and allows them to trial correct procedures with close supervision. Trainers may then suggest behavioural or operating adjustments, gradually releasing responsibility to the worker to continue on their own using safer practices. This will result in fewer workplace injuries, further reducing this key performance indicator at Manitta Mining and contributing to achievement of its objective to improve workplace safety.

This question asks for an 'examination', meaning you will need to explore various aspects. As there are three allocated marks, you can assume this means at least three points should be made or aspects discussed. 'Examine' can be addressed by illustrating how and why something may be done. Don't forget to link back to the case study and stimulus. Note carefully that although three Study Design terms can be found in this question, there are no marks allocated for definitions.

**Mark breakdown:**
- 1 mark for referring to the number of workplace accidents
- 1 mark for linking staff training to reducing the number of workplace accidents
- 1 mark for linking specific types of staff training to reducing the number of workplace accidents at Manitta Mining

**c** It is very important to review key performance indicators to measure the effectiveness of business transformation. The aim should be to ensure plans that have been made are being implemented and to the set timeline, that employees and managers are maintaining changed behaviours or practices, and that the results are as per the forecast desired outcomes. Manitta Mining wanted to reduce the number of workplace accidents, so first it had to research the initial data, then make a plan to improve the situation and finally review any change over time to compare to the original measure. Once a data comparison is made, managers could base their decisions on that evidence to make further change, maintain that course of action or resolve to wait for more data before taking further steps. The CEO of Manitta Mining states that 'a key business objective is to improve workplace safety'. Without keeping track of the number of workplace accidents, the business will not be able to monitor change over time or know whether it has effectively achieved its overall business transformation goal or whether further corrective action is required, so this performance indicator must be reviewed regularly.

As an 'explain' question, you need to show the potential impact of reviewing key performance indicators to measure business transformation. Some comment needs to be made about the importance of doing this, and you must mention how Manitta Mining might use data collected. As the question stipulates effectiveness, this needs to be specifically addressed in your response. It is good to use a relevant short quote from the stimulus to show how closely your answer links to the scenario, and this could well gain you a mark. However, ensure you only use snippets so you don't waste test time copying or using up too much of your available writing space.

**Mark breakdown:**
- 2 marks for considering the importance of measurement of change using key performance indicators
- 1 mark for linking to measuring the effectiveness of business transformation
- 1 mark for linking to Manitta Mining scenario

## Question 6

A real-life example demonstrating both sides of considering corporate social responsibility when implementing change is Melbourne-founded fashion brand Forever New.

The textiles industry is now known to use unsustainable and unsafe production methods, exploit workers and create end-product landfill waste. If Forever New is to attract its target market of younger female customers, who are well educated and often care deeply about our environment and social issues, then the business needs to demonstrate commitment to making positive change in its industry.

Forever New advertises aspects of corporate social responsibility on its home page, such as having dedicated committees to oversee diversity and inclusion, culture and wellbeing, sustainability and the environment. Its 'Conscious' clothing range contains at least 30% responsible fibres (lower environmental impact), or is produced with environmentally responsible processes. The business aims for fashion to make a more meaningful contribution to industry, culture, communities and the environment. It operates under five 'pillars of change', including reducing its environmental footprint, sourcing ethical suppliers and forming charity partnerships. These strategies act to reassure customers that they are making more sustainable fashion purchases and so may increase the number of customers, market share and number of sales.

However, implementing these policies and programs comes at a cost to the business. Sourcing ethical suppliers, using lower impact fibres and paying fair manufacturer wages increases input expenses and takes time, effort and expertise to manage. Forever New management would need to commit more financial and human resources than its less environmentally friendly competitors, and products may end up costing more for the end consumer. The business must make decisions about which course of action is more in line with its corporate values and more likely to attract its target customers. If Forever New chooses not to work towards fashion production change, the business may lose customers and damage its reputation, resulting in lower profits. It may be worth paying more initially for inputs to respond to changing social attitudes, if customers are more brand-loyal, or spend more on 'conscious' products, resulting in higher profits in the long term.

Source: https://www.forevernew.com.au/forever-conscious

This is a 'discuss' question and so it is expected that you provide aspects of both sides of something – in this case the impact on a real-life business if it does or doesn't take account of corporate social responsibility. You might know a case study that does act in a socially responsible way, but you may not know the details of what it's doing (or not doing). In this case, it's fine to take an educated guess and write about potential issues, as long as you link appropriately to your chosen business.

**Mark breakdown:**
- 2 marks for business outcomes of considering corporate social responsibility using an appropriate real-life example
- 2 marks for business outcomes of not considering corporate social responsibility using an appropriate real-life example

# TEST 11: IMPLEMENTING CHANGE

## Question 1

Corporate culture is the beliefs, values, ideas and expectations shared by people within a business. It can influence the ways people behave and interact with each other and can be communicated in various ways, such as written documents and visual elements (e.g. logo).

It is important that your definition is detailed and contains at least two distinctive parts, features or characteristics related to the concept. In this case, the first distinctive characteristic relates to shared values and beliefs and the second characteristic is that it influences behaviour and communication.

**Mark breakdown:**
- 1 mark for characteristic(s) of the term
- 1 mark for detail or relevant example(s)

## Question 2

Oscar and Aroha can improve corporate culture by revising and updating the vision, mission and values in the official documentation of Lakeside Health to acknowledge the modernisation of the medical clinic for various stakeholders. By aligning the vision, service provision processes, work practices and symbols, corporate culture can be improved by creating a sense of shared goals, pride and connectedness for employees to the multiple changes that have been introduced. When employees feel a sense of pride and connectedness to the vision, mission and values of a business, they are more likely to have higher morale, which subsequently has a positive impact on corporate culture.

There are many strategies that can be suggested to improve corporate culture. Other suggestions may include (but are not limited to) training and development, the introduction of rituals or celebrations, changing the dominant management style, using rewards, effective communication or changing shared language.

**Mark breakdown:**
- 1 mark for suggesting a logical strategy to improve corporate culture at Lakeside Health
- 2 marks for providing supporting reason(s) for how the suggested strategy can improve corporate culture at Lakeside Health

**Top tip**
The key to effectively answering this question is to suggest a strategy where you can logically link the justification to the stimulus material. In the sample answer, the justification provides a detailed link between updating official documentation and the introduction of the new changes.

## Question 3

To create a positive culture for change, Oscar and Aroha can apply Senge's Learning Organisation principles of systems thinking and personal mastery.

Because there are multiple changes being introduced with new online technologies, new equipment and renovations, it is essential for Oscar and Aroha to apply systems thinking in order to consider the 'big picture'. Systems thinking sees all parts of the business as interrelated, affecting each other and connected as a whole. It will assist Oscar and Aroha to see patterns of connection between different areas of the business across inputs, processes and outputs (such as bookings, diagnostic capabilities during appointments and overall customer experience), rather than the parts in isolation. To create a positive culture for change, systems thinking will help to guide the change process with a long-term view, through implementing strategies and actions that are synchronised and complementary, rather than disconnected, disjointed or short term.

The new online technologies and diagnostic equipment that are being introduced will require staff to undergo training to ensure they have the knowledge and skills necessary to competently implement the change in technology. The application of personal mastery will create the conditions necessary to ensure that individual employees are personally committed to developing their ability to gain and apply new skills, focus their energy and continually strive to achieve their personal vision for their work. When individual employees improve their performance through a personal commitment to learning, employees collectively improve and work towards the achievement of business objectives, and subsequently, the overall culture of the business improves.

There are five principles of the Learning Organisation: systems thinking, personal mastery, mental models, building a shared vision and team learning. All the principles can be applied to create a positive culture for change at Lakeside Health; however, only two are required to gain full marks.

**Mark breakdown (global marking):**
- 1–2 marks for identifying one or two Learning Organisation principles and outlining them briefly
- 3–4 marks for outlining two relevant Learning Organisation principles and detailing how Oscar and Aroha can apply the principles at Lakeside Health to create a positive culture for change, with some detail
- 5–6 marks for outlining two relevant Learning Organisation principles and thoroughly detailing how Oscar and Aroha can apply the principles at Lakeside Health to create a positive culture for change

## Question 4

To implement change successfully, Oscar and Aroha will need to act as leaders and empower their employees to navigate the changes from the existing conditions to an upgraded and modernised Lakeside Health medical clinic. Overall, the 2025–2027 data demonstrates declining performance in all areas measured, so as leaders Oscar and Aroha will need to have a clear vision for the future and communicate that vision effectively to staff and other stakeholders, such as customers.

In response to declining appointments and website hits, Oscar and Aroha have demonstrated their willingness to seek out new ideas and upgrade their processes, equipment and premises. To successfully improve net profit figures following a period of decline, it will be important for them to actively promote the change and build a sense of confidence with stakeholders. They will also need to ensure that staff are well-trained in order to minimise disruption and improve customer satisfaction with the clinic. Staff turnover has increased from 5% in 2026 to 15% in 2027; this is concerning and may indicate low staff morale, which could cause resistance to the changes. To overcome resistance and restore staff turnover to a lower level, Oscar and Aroha will need to seek feedback from staff during the change process and reward supportive behaviours.

When you are planning your response to a question like this, a useful approach is to identify the characteristics of leadership and then consider the impact that each characteristic has on the different areas of the business addressed in the key performance indicators. The importance of leadership is then emphasised when the link between a characteristic of leadership and the effect on the key performance indicator is made clear. Use the statistics from the stimulus material to ensure close links. 'Analyse' asks you to demonstrate how various parts impact the whole.

**Mark breakdown:**
- 1 mark for detailing the characteristic(s) of leadership during this period of change at Lakeside Health
- 1 mark for outlining the importance of leadership during this period of change at Lakeside Health
- 2 marks for linking the impact leadership would have during this period of change at Lakeside Health to at least two key performance indicators

## Question 5

Both employees and customers of Lakeside Health may need to overcome initial resistance to change and move towards acceptance of the upgraded technology, equipment and premises. For employees, resistance may be due to fear of redundancy or redeployment, or concerns about not being capable of learning new skills. Customers may resist as they may be put off by the disruptions caused by the renovations, or may feel confused about whether the clinic is still offering previous services.

The employees and customers will both need to learn how to use the new booking system and adapt their habits or expectations about the booking processes accordingly; however, their training needs are different. Employees will require training and support to learn how to use the new systems to serve customers. However, customers will not receive formal training other than online or verbal instructions, and those who dislike using technology or prefer to book appointments in person may need additional support and instruction from employees about navigating the new booking process, responding to SMS reminders or accessing the on-demand telehealth service.

It can be challenging to think of similarities between two stakeholders that are as different as employees and customers. When planning this response, try to think logically about human nature; regardless of who the stakeholder is, consider what each stakeholder might struggle with during a time of change. In this scenario, focusing on challenges relating to new technologies and adapting to new processes or practices are issues that the owners would need to anticipate in their planning for both employees and customers.

**Mark breakdown:**
- 2 marks for providing potential similarities
- 2 marks for providing potential differences

## Question 6

When employees are empowered, they are more likely to have increased positive impact as they contribute to implementation of the new technologies and adjust to the renovations, which can help to overcome resistance to change. Empowerment is a strategy that can increase morale and productivity as employees are trusted to take more responsibility for autonomous decision-making and the way they adapt to the changes. Being more involved in the change process can create a stronger culture of commitment to ensuring the success of the change in both the short and long term. Empowerment can also improve staff retention, which would make it an effective low-risk strategy for Lakeside Health to consider, given the unwanted increase in staff turnover in 2027.

However, due to how costly the new technologies and renovation will have been for Oscar and Aroha, empowerment could prove to be a risky strategy when employees lack sufficient skills and experience, as mistakes or poor decisions could be made. A lack of clear guidance or direction could also decrease efficiency, due to a lack of coordinated efforts between the employees and the resulting unnecessary rework. Increasing autonomy and responsibility through empowerment might also blur professional relationships or lead to accountability issues. Without a clear vision, transparency and effective communication, empowerment can lead to confusion or even conflict, so positive leadership from Aroha and Oscar will be essential.

Overall, empowerment is an effective low-risk strategy to overcome employee resistance to the introduction of this business change, when it is coupled with positive leadership, open and transparent communication and a clear vision for how the changes will positively transform and improve Lakeside Health.

While there is some detail provided in the scenario, including key performance indicators, answering a question like this involves making a number of assumptions, such as about the culture of the clinic, the challenges that might arise during the change process and the dominant management style of Oscar and Aroha. To gain full marks, it is necessary to flesh out in enough detail the advantages and disadvantages and conclude with a logical opinion.

**Mark breakdown:**
- 2 marks for advantages of the use of empowerment
- 2 marks for disadvantages of the use of empowerment
- 1 mark for a logical opinion based on the advantages and disadvantages presented

## Question 7

a   The gradual decline in the total number of appointments and website hits can indicate issues relating to the quality of the services provided by Lakeside Health. Focusing on improving the quality of services can help to improve business performance in the future. One of the ways Oscar and Aroha could do this is through implementing a quality strategy such as Total Quality Management, sharing the responsibility for continuous improvement in service quality with all their employees. Having the administration team and practitioners focused on the customers, acting on customer feedback to improve systems and committed to excellence may help to improve the quality of all aspects of the services provided.

While the question does not ask for a definition, you need to demonstrate that you understand what the strategy entails in order to adequately describe how an application of the strategy could improve certain key performance indicators in the future.

**Mark breakdown:**
- 1 mark for outlining a quality strategy
- 2 marks for detailing how the implementation of the strategy can improve at least one of the key performance indicators at Lakeside Health

**b** Staff training involves improving the knowledge and skills of employees so they perform their jobs more efficiently and effectively. Improving the performance of staff through investing in training can address a number of concerns when it comes to business performance. Improved customer service could increase the total number of appointments, which would subsequently increase net profit figures through increasing sales and could also increase net profit figures by reducing errors and waste. The increase in staff turnover may indicate low job satisfaction among staff, so investing in training may improve motivation and strengthen employee commitment to Lakeside Health, thus positively impacting staff turnover.

Once again, although the question does not ask for a definition, you need to demonstrate you understand what the strategy entails in order to adequately describe how an application of the strategy could improve certain key performance indicators in the future.

**Mark breakdown:**
- 1 mark for outlining a training strategy
- 2 marks for detailing how the implementation of the strategy can improve at least one of the key performance indicators at Lakeside Health

# TEST 12: UNIT 4

**Question 1**

**a**  **i** Number of website hits measures the number of visitors to the website of a business over a specific period of time. Alliance Real Estate could use this indicator to measure the level of engagement and how well it is attracting people to the new innovations on the website. This would provide valuable insight into whether its investment into specific strategies, such as the online sales platform, has resulted in increased website traffic.

  **ii** Percentage of market share represents the portion of total industry sales earned by Alliance Real Estate expressed as a percentage. Alliance Real Estate can use percentage of market share to assess the degree to which its investment in various online platforms and software has resulted in an increase in sales, and whether this has improved its competitive advantage.

When answering a question like this, you gain the second mark for each key performance indicator by including specific and related details from the scenario.

**Mark breakdown:**
- 1 mark for outlining what the key performance indicator measures
- 1 mark for detailing how Alliance Real Estate can use the key performance indicator to measure business performance, with links to the scenario

**b** Labour resources are provided by people through the mental and physical efforts exerted in the production process. New business opportunities have been sought by changing the way the sales and administrative teams perform their jobs, rearranging and reallocating labour resources (employees) to perform different tasks and activities, and using new technologies, instead of employees, to produce real estate sales as outputs.

While the sample answer focuses on the redeployment of labour resources, an alternative response could outline how Alliance Real Estate sought new business opportunities by rearranging or redistributing capital resources such as changing its office layout, updating audiovisual equipment or reducing the corporate vehicle fleet.

**Mark breakdown:**
- 1 mark for briefly describing the concept of redeployment of resources (capital or labour)
- 1 mark for detailing how Alliance Real Estate has used the strategy to seek new business opportunities

c   Alliance Real Estate is aiming to take advantage of new business opportunities by investing in innovative technologies to meet interstate and overseas customer demand for regional properties. By applying the principles of the Force Field Analysis, the manager of Alliance Real Estate can determine the forces that are going to drive or resist change, in order to develop a plan to guide the desired change.

The first key principle is to identify the current driving and restraining forces relating to implementing innovative technologies to target Melbourne, interstate and overseas buyers. An example of a driving force may be societal attitudes, such as buyers wanting the convenience of viewing and purchasing property online. A relevant restraining force may be financial considerations such as the cost of buying software licences.

Ranking is the second principle, which would involve the manager prioritising the top driving forces to be strengthened and the most dominant restraining forces to be eliminated or minimised. For Alliance Real Estate, the manager may identify innovation as a driving force to be strengthened and legislation around legally compliant contracts as a restraining force to be minimised.

The third principle involves developing an action plan and implementing an appropriate response. To do this, the manager will need to allocate roles and responsibilities for each action, such as the sales staff now having to meet targets for virtual sales.

The last principle is for Alliance Real Estate to evaluate the response, by assessing the degree to which the change has been successful. This can be done through assessing key performance indicators such as net profit figures, number of virtual sales and number of website hits.

When planning a response where you 'apply' a theory to a business scenario, it is useful to structure the response in a way that mimics the order of the theory. For the Force Field Analysis, start with weighting, then apply the principle of ranking, detail the implementation of the response and conclude with how the business would evaluate. Paragraphs can help you ensure you cover all required parts and make it easy to check whether you have provided enough detail to be awarded the marks.

**Mark breakdown:**
- 1 mark for detailing how the principle 'weighting' may have been applied at Alliance Real Estate
- 1 mark for detailing how the principle 'ranking' may have been applied at Alliance Real Estate
- 1 mark for detailing how the principle 'implementing a response' may have been applied at Alliance Real Estate
- 1 mark for detailing how the principle 'evaluating' may have been applied at Alliance Real Estate

d   Innovation improves on existing processes and practices through adapting to new or creative ideas. Innovation has been a driving force for change at Alliance Real Estate, as the business is adapting to changes in the external environment by identifying some niche markets (in this case Melbourne, interstate and overseas property buyers) and implementing new technological advancements to respond to the needs of the target markets. Innovating and using technology to implement new ways of selling properties can give Alliance Real Estate a competitive advantage, thus encouraging making the change.

Another driving force that may have influenced change at Alliance Real Estate is societal attitudes. In the past, many would have found it inconceivable to buy property without being physically present. However, with shifts in societal values and attitudes towards purchasing goods and services online, 3D technology and increased trust in terms of privacy, people are becoming more accepting of new technologies to facilitate the sale and purchase of properties, also encouraging this business to change.

From the driving forces listed in the Study Design, the only two driving forces that would not be acceptable responses would be pursuit of profit, because it is not mentioned in the question, and legislation, as there is no detail included that would indicate changes in legislation have acted as a driving force.

**Mark breakdown:**
- 1 mark for identifying and detailing a relevant driving force for Alliance Real Estate (× 2)
- 1 mark for detailing how the selected driving force might have influenced change at Alliance Real Estate (× 2)

**e**  By catering to increased demand for regional and overseas clients, Alliance Real Estate may be contributing to the local economy through attracting wealthier homeowners into the local community, which may boost the local economy for other businesses. A disadvantage of doing this is that as supply lessens, housing prices in the local community increase, which may make it too expensive for local people to be able to afford to buy or rent properties in the area in which they have always lived.

If Alliance Real Estate is successful and can increase its percentage of market share and net profit figures, then it may need to hire more people from the local community to expand its operations. A downside of this is that its growth and success may negatively impact other real estate businesses in the community by reducing competition, decreasing business performance of competitors, or through the poaching of staff. Further, as Alliance Real Estate has invested in online technologies, the manager may outsource some operations; the agency doesn't necessarily have to hire staff from the local community, but outsourcing may increase local unemployment.

Ultimately, the extent to which Alliance Real Estate positively or negatively impacts the general community will largely depend on the decisions made by management about the ways in which they support and participate in the local economy and community. Provided Alliance Real Estate employs local people and supports the local economy through attracting customers to spend in local businesses, the general community should benefit from its success overall.

This question is a challenging one, as a number of assumptions need to be made about the potential positive and negative impacts on the local community and economy through selling local properties to interstate and overseas clients using innovative technologies. The social and economic impacts of change on the general community as a stakeholder can be more challenging to explain than the environmental impacts. This highlights the importance of studying a range of contemporary case studies from different industries and communities to broaden your understanding of the diverse ways stakeholders may be affected by change.

**Mark breakdown:**
- 2 marks for strengths
- 2 marks for weaknesses
- 1 mark for an overall opinion, supported by key ideas presented in the response and linked to Alliance Real Estate

**Top tip**
In this response, the first strength is presented and the related weakness is weighed against the key point outlined in the opening sentence to the paragraph. This approach is replicated in the next paragraph. Structuring the response in this way instead of clustering the strengths together and the weaknesses together can be read as a more sophisticated evaluation. However, always be sure to clearly explain why the same action or situation could be both a strength and a weakness.

**f**  An appropriate low-risk strategy Alliance Real Estate could implement is incentives. To encourage employees to be more on-board with change or new ways of doing things, incentives can be offered in different ways, such as bonuses, promotions, opportunities for additional responsibility or performance-related pay. Because Alliance Real Estate generates sales through selling properties, incentivising staff during the process of adapting to new technologies and new methods for converting customer interest into sales may be an effective way to overcome resistance to change, as incentives directly link effort and enthusiasm to a tangible reward.

While threats need to be used with caution, threats can be used by a manager to exert force on an employee to overcome resistance to change. Because there are multiple changes being implemented at Alliance Real Estate simultaneously, such as changes to job descriptions and office layout, it is possible the manager may resort to issuing threats of redundancy or demotion as a short-term strategy to get the employees on board and implement changes more quickly. However, threats are a high-risk strategy as they can erode trust and may ultimately lead to more employee resistance in the long term.

In a stimulus scenario such as Alliance Real Estate, any of the low-risk and high-risk strategies listed in the Study Design could be proposed to overcome employee resistance to change. Further options include communication, empowerment, support and manipulation.

**Mark breakdown:**
- 1 mark for suggesting a relevant strategy to overcome employee resistance to change at Alliance Real Estate (× 2)
- 2 marks for defending the selection of each strategy as a means to overcome employee resistance to change, with links to the scenario (× 2)

**Top tip**

In an industry such as real estate, it is common practice for employees to be incentivised with performance-related pay based on the level of sales they achieve as an individual or team, so using this realistic example in a response demonstrates a good level of business awareness.

## Question 2

*The following is an actual student response taken from the 2019 examiners' report.*

Peter Senge stated that Learning Organisations are those businesses where managers and employees continually seek to improve and achieve their desired results. There are five principles that must be present in order to have a learning organisation: systems thinking, mental models, shared vision, personal mastery and team learning.

In order to effectively manage employees during a period of change, managers could apply the principle of personal mastery. Individuals show continual development towards achieving the vision they set for themselves. This could be done through providing employees with training in order to develop their proficiency and allow manages to successfully apply this principle. This will work towards successful change as managers are working with employees to ensure they can perform their work to the highest possible standard. However, applying personal mastery for every employee may become time consuming and counterproductive towards managing employees.

To positively influence corporate culture, a business going through change could apply a shared vision (developing a vision every person in the business believes in) and team learning (developing capacity and ability of a team to create results members truly desire). This could involve providing regular communication to ensure employees understand the vision. Having a vision that everyone believes in will develop genuine commitment, as employees believe in the purpose of the business, leading to a positive influence on corporate culture. Team learning will enable employees to develop relationships within the business, therefore there is a positive relationship between team learning and corporate culture.

A business could apply mental models (deeply ingrained assumptions) and systems thinking (viewing bigger picture of business, not events in isolation) to ensure change is implemented successfully. A business could challenge the mental models of employees to help them accept and embrace change and become less resistant. Systems thinking, as the cornerstone of the learning organisation, could help to implement change successfully as managers can see how the change may impact different areas of the business. To do this, however, may be time consuming to audit different areas of a business to see how the change could impact the business as a whole, in order to ensure successful change.

Source: *VCAA 2019 VCE Business Management examination report*

Before you start writing an extended response worth 10 marks, it is advisable to make a brief plan for how to tackle the question. In this response, there are three key contexts relating to change (managing employees, corporate culture and successful implementation). Each context needs to be addressed when applying the principles of Senge's Learning Organisation theory. In the sample response, each context has its own paragraph. The main body of each paragraph has at least one principle linked to the context presented and coverage of the five principles is achieved across the three main body paragraphs. Planning the response in this way makes it easier for the assessor to determine the degree to which the question has been answered and award marks accordingly. Always try to make your responses easy to follow and mark.

For further detail on this past examination question, see the *2019 VCE Business Management examination report* on the VCAA website.

**Mark breakdown (global marking):**
- 1–3 marks for limited detail regarding the application of the principles of Senge's Learning Organisation during change, with limited reference to managing employees, corporate culture and successful implementation
- 4–7 marks for some detail regarding the application of the principles of Senge's Learning Organisation during change, with some reference to managing employees, corporate culture and successful implementation
- 8–10 marks for thorough application of the principles of Senge's Learning Organisation during change, with detailed reference to managing employees, corporate culture and successful implementation

## Question 3

**a** Business change involves any modification to the internal or external environment of a business, usually through the adoption of a new idea or a new way of doing things. Shandra's Dairy Ltd is embarking on business change in a number of ways, such as implementing a new quality strategy (change in behaviour) and diversifying into the global snack food market (adoption of a new idea).

To expand on a generic description of the concept of business change, include specific examples of business change at Shandra's Dairy Ltd from the case study.

**Mark breakdown:**
- 1 mark for providing the characteristics of business change
- 1 mark for detailing business change in the context of Shandra's Dairy Ltd, with links to the scenario

**b** Shandra's Dairy Ltd is choosing to initiate change, in anticipation of how it can adapt to changing circumstances, and therefore is taking a proactive approach to change. While Shandra's Dairy Ltd already has quality control in place, it is planning to implement a second quality strategy to achieve a higher degree of excellence prior to diversification. Also, while the business is a successful Australian dairy with a growing percentage of market share, diversification into another market is identified as necessary in order to become a global brand. Planning and initiating such a significant change, when there is no data to suggest the business needs to diversify to address a pressing issue, indicates proactive change is being undertaken.

The final example from the case study relates to environmental sustainability. While it is acknowledged that the changes to renewable energy are aligned with the Australian Government's Renewable Energy Target, Shandra's Dairy Ltd appears to be motivated by a genuine commitment to being environmentally sustainable. This is supported by the significant investment into multiple strategies to make the site self-sufficient for the long term. As these changes are not in response to overt pressure from the government or other interest groups to act in a certain way, this is a proactive approach rather than reactive.

In the case of Shandra's Dairy Ltd, there is little information in the case study that indicates that the business is being reactive in its approach to change. Rather, it appears to be initiating a series of changes to improve performance across different aspects of the business. Therefore, it is most logical that the approach to change is proactive.

**Mark breakdown:**
- 1 mark to identify that the change is proactive
- 3 marks for providing supporting sources of evidence from the case study to demonstrate that the change at Shandra's Dairy Ltd is proactive

c   The first strategy the managers of Shandra's Dairy Ltd could implement to strengthen corporate culture is to change the milking staff uniforms to be made of 100% recycled materials. This change is aligned with Shandra's Dairy Ltd's commitment to environmental sustainability and, if labelled, visually demonstrates the business-wide commitment to reducing environmental impact. It can also engender a sense of pride for employees when they physically wear the uniform while milking the cows.

A second strategy the managers could implement to strengthen corporate culture would be to reward staff who demonstrate appropriate values relating to environmental sustainability. This could be through the creation of a volunteer or charity program, an environmental sustainability initiative suggestion box or offering incentives for those who run initiatives relating to sustainability, such as recycling, feed packaging or clean-up-the-farm days. Celebrating exemplary behaviours relating to environmental sustainability can improve employee connectedness and strengthen the positive reputation of Shandra's Dairy Ltd.

> Introducing new uniforms and rewarding staff who demonstrate exemplary values are not unique environmental sustainability strategies. However, by framing the implementation of both as strategies to symbolically and tangibly engender a business-wide commitment to environmental sustainability, Shandra's Dairy Ltd can apply both to strengthen corporate culture.
>
> **Mark breakdown:**
> - 1 mark for identifying and detailing a strategy relevant to Shandra's Dairy Ltd and related to environmental sustainability (× 2)
> - 1 mark for demonstrating how Shandra's Dairy Ltd can use the strategy to improve corporate culture relating to environmental sustainability (× 2)

d   The Three-step Change Model is a theory that provides a framework for managing business change. Unfreeze is the first step. It involves preparing the business to undergo change by first identifying what needs to change, then building momentum towards changing the status quo. At Shandra's Dairy Ltd, the unfreeze step will need to consist of communicating the vision and benefits for diversification into the snack food market to key stakeholders to bring them on board, within a 3-year period. Then Shandra's Dairy Ltd will need to allay any concerns or doubt about the vision or change process to gain energy towards the desired change.

The second step comes once Shandra's Dairy Ltd is unfrozen. To move the business towards the desired state, diversifying into the snack food market, management will need to implement the change. This is done through directing resources towards the change efforts, providing ongoing support to stakeholders, preparing for the transition into the new market and empowering employees to implement the change successfully. During this stage, regular and clear communication to dispel rumours and address concerns is necessary to reduce resistance and ensure the diversification strategy is achieved successfully.

To reinforce the change, the last step in the change process is refreeze. Refreeze is necessary to anchor the change into the policies, processes and practices of Shandra's Dairy Ltd. This last stage ensures the culture of Shandra's Dairy Ltd is reflective of the diverse range of dairy and snack food products manufactured by Shandra's Dairy Ltd. Further support and training will be necessary to ensure consistency and stability when operating in the snack food market. Creating opportunities for staff to contribute to ongoing innovation and celebrating successes will help to maintain momentum.

During the period of change, it is necessary for managers to be minimising the impact of restraining forces that may hinder Shandra's Dairy Ltd's efforts to become a truly global brand.

Organisational inertia could be described as working in a 'comfort zone' or maintaining the 'status quo'. Given Shandra's Dairy Ltd is one of the largest independent dairies in Australia and is currently increasing its percentage of market share, it is feasible there will be people within the business who may disagree with diversifying into the snack food market. These employees may use tactics such as avoidance, stalling or a lack of commitment as a means of keeping the business operating in a way that they feel is safe and predictable. If this is the case, organisational inertia could act as a restraining force against Shandra's Dairy Ltd diversifying.

While it is stated that the manufacturing of snack foods could be done on existing machinery and by sourcing raw materials from existing suppliers, diversifying and exporting to over 20 countries would still require a significant financial investment. Potential costs include retraining employees, changing the layout of the manufacturing facilities, purchasing raw materials, paying high international shipping costs, as well as losing productivity for the dairy while resources are used to produce potato chips. Therefore, financial considerations can act as a restraining force when all costs and benefits are analysed, and this long-term cost of the change poses a risk.

When reading and responding to this question, it can be broken down into two parts: application of the Three-step Change Model and consideration of two restraining forces.

The question does not require a definition of each step when writing about the Three-step Change Model. However, in order to apply each step accurately, you do need to demonstrate you understand what the steps would entail at Shandra's Dairy Ltd. Note the use of three clear paragraphs to address the three-part theory.

To effectively answer the part of the question relating to restraining forces, you can anticipate potential challenges posed by two restraining forces in the change process at Shandra's Dairy Ltd. The sample response considers corporate culture (linked to organisational inertia) and the significant expense associated with diversification (linked to financial considerations). Including reasonable assumptions about what may occur at Shandra's Dairy Ltd is a strategy you can use to bring depth to your explanation of each restraining force.

**Marking guide (global marking):**
- 1–3 marks for a limited description of the Three-step Change Model and two restraining forces, with links to Shandra's Dairy Ltd addressed briefly or not addressed
- 4–7 marks for detailed consideration of the Three-step Change Model and two restraining forces, with links to Shandra's Dairy Ltd addressed with some detail
- 8–10 marks for sophisticated consideration of the Three-step Change Model and two restraining forces, with links to Shandra's Dairy Ltd addressed in a thorough manner

e *The following is an actual student response taken from the 2017 examiners' report.*
The differentiation approach is where the business is able to gain a stable competitive advantage by becoming unique in its industry in a way that is valued by customers. Shandra's Dairy Ltd should differentiate their dairy products by giving them unique value, which could be done by using unique ingredients and recipes for their dairy products which are unmatched by competitors in the industry. By having a unique dairy range which customers value, Shandra's Dairy Ltd will be able to develop a highly loyal customer base and demand for their products as customers are unable to get the unique items from competitors. This approach, if done correctly, will allow for Shandra's Dairy Ltd to charge a premium price for their products, as customers are willing to pay more as they perceive their dairy products to be of special value. This will allow for Shandra's Dairy Ltd to increase their profits on each sale made. However, Shandra's Dairy Ltd may find that they run into cost issues in their attempts to add value to their products. If costs rise uncontrollably, the benefit of premium pricing will be negated. Also, if a competitor decides to copy the products produced by Shandra's Dairy Ltd, they may lose their unique attributes and therefore run the risk of no longer being unique.

Source: *VCAA 2017 Business Management examination report*

This response used Porter's Generic Strategy of differentiation well. It was closely linked to the case study stimulus material and logical assumptions made with business impacts noted.

For further detail on this past examination question, see the 2017 VCE Business Management examination report on the VCAA website.

**Marking guide (global marking):**
- 1 mark for identifying Porter's lower cost or differentiation approach linked to Shandra's Dairy Ltd
- 2 marks for providing advantages
- 2 marks for providing disadvantages

**f**   Organisational inertia could also be described as working in a 'comfort zone', or maintaining the 'status quo'. Given Shandra's Dairy Ltd is one of the largest independent dairies in Australia and is currently increasing its percentage of market share, it is feasible there will be people within the business who may disagree with diversifying into the snack food market. These employees may use tactics such as avoidance, stalling or a lack of commitment as a means of keeping the business operating in a way they feel is safe and predictable. In this case, organisational inertia could act as a restraining force against Shandra's Dairy Ltd diversifying.

While it is stated the manufacturing of snack foods could be done on existing machinery and by sourcing raw materials from existing suppliers, diversification and exporting to over 20 countries would still require a significant financial investment. Potential costs include retraining employees, changing the layout of the manufacturing facilities, purchasing raw materials and paying high international shipping costs, as well as losing productivity for the dairy while resources are used to produce potato chips. Therefore, financial considerations can act as a restraining force when all costs and benefits are analysed and this long-term cost of the change poses risk.

> To effectively answer this question, you can anticipate potential challenges the change process may cause at Shandra's Dairy Ltd relating to corporate culture (linked to organisational inertia) and the significant expense associated with diversification (linked to financial considerations). Including reasonable assumptions about what may occur at Shandra's Dairy Ltd is a strategy you can use to bring depth to your explanation of each restraining force.
>
> **Mark breakdown:**
> - 1 mark for outlining in detail the concept of organisational inertia
> - 1 mark for detailing how organisational inertia may work against changes implemented at Shandra's Dairy Ltd
> - 1 mark for outlining in detail the concept of financial considerations
> - 1 mark for detailing how financial considerations may work against changes implemented at Shandra's Dairy Ltd

# PRACTICE EXAM 1

## SECTION A

**Question 1**

**a**   Sole traders are owned and operated by one person, such as Sarah working by herself on *Go for it*. Sole traders assume all liability for business debts and have full control of all business decisions.

> **Marking guide:**
> - 1 mark for feature(s) of a sole trader
> - 1 mark for added detail or example(s) linked to *Go for it*

**b**   One key performance indicator relevant to *Go for it* would be the number of website hits, which shows how many times people have clicked on the public-facing webpage. This data may need close analysis, as website hits could come from many different people, or they could be from a few people visiting multiple times. Website hits may be visits by potential or current customers.

A second relevant key performance indicator would be percentage of market share. This is the number of sales in a particular market – in this case in the online training and coaching industry – that a business has in relation to its competitors and is expressed as a percentage. Sarah Shine's percentage of market share must be growing, because recent sales have increased by 60%.

> **Marking guide:**
> - 2 marks for providing characteristics of a relevant indicator linked to *Go for it* (× 2)

**c**   There are various global considerations that Sarah needs to take into account if hiring employees working in another country. There are advantages, such as being able to comply with overseas labour laws, which may allow less-expensive human resource costs, and access to highly skilled or experienced candidates who may not be available in Sarah's local community.

However, there are disadvantages. For example, as owner, Sarah will need to ensure that she retains full decision-making power and knows how her employees are behaving while representing her business. This may be difficult to do if her assistant is in Brazil and there could be a negative impact on her business reputation if poor decisions are made, customers are not treated well or business systems are not followed. Another disadvantage of having a remote team is the challenge of building relationships to develop effective teamwork, particularly if outsourced employees are from different ethnic cultures. Face-to-face presence allows for incidental relationship-building that benefits the overall work culture, and hiring local employees ensures some shared understanding.

> **Marking guide:**
> - 2 marks for advantages of global outsourcing linked to *Go for it*
> - 2 marks for disadvantages of global outsourcing linked to *Go for it*

**d**   When building a remote working team, Sarah can use the consultative management style. The consultative style uses the kind of two-way communication that will be essential to achieving business objectives while working separately. Without close supervision, remote workers need to be trusted to manage their own workload. The consultative style allows for Sarah, as the manager, to check in with employees, set targets and then allow them to get on with the work and report back. The effective communication of the consultative style provides increased transparency and autonomy within the team, giving employees some ownership over decision-making; however, Sarah retains the ultimate authority. Employees feel empowered, increase their job satisfaction, and are also well-supported, as Sarah consults them for their input but then guides the overall business direction.

**Marking guide:**
- 1 mark for suggesting a suitable management style
- 2 marks for explaining why the selected style is appropriate
- 1 mark for extended detail with close references to *Go for it*

**e**  On-the-job training refers to professional development for new employees while they are at work.

This may be a suitable choice for Sarah's business as on-the-job training can be cost-effective, especially if she conducts the training herself, and allows productivity to continue as employees are working while they learn. The familiar environment allows workers to feel comfortable as they learn, and Sarah is able to tailor training to her specific business needs, such as using particular software or equipment.

However, if Sarah chooses to be the trainer, she may not be across current best-practice business solutions, such as software or hosting platforms that would improve her business performance. Sarah also may not have the expertise needed to effectively lead professional learning, and her own work would decrease while she is leading training.

Despite these challenges, as Sarah understands her business vision and systems well, on-the-job training might be more efficient than new workers going to an external consultant who doesn't know the business.

**Marking guide:**
- 1 mark for benefit(s) of on-the-job training
- 1 mark for limitation(s) of on-the-job training
- 1 mark for assessment of suitability for the particular scenario at *Go for it*

## Question 2

**a**  The concept of business change refers to the transformation businesses must go through to keep operating effectively and efficiently in the dynamic business environment. For example, businesses may take a quality management approach of continuous improvement through small, incremental changes that are everyone's responsibility, and which all add up to major change over time and across multiple business functions to keep the business competitive.

**Marking guide:**
- 1 mark for providing characteristics of business change
- 1 mark for providing an appropriate example of the concept in practice

**b**  Manipulation and threat are both high-risk strategies when trying to overcome employee resistance to change. This is because both strategies can result in employees becoming fearful or resentful towards the manager, losing loyalty to the business and possibly leaving to find a more collegiate workplace. Both strategies can work for the short term in times of crisis, but only if the manager has already developed a good working relationship with employees and they can trust that it is only a temporary tactic.

The difference between the terms is that manipulation involves only giving employees select information, or bounded choices, to ensure they take a predetermined course of action, whereas threat does not involve any pretence of choice, with a manager coercing employees by threatening some aspect of their employment if something is not done. Threats can be direct or indirect and involve giving employees an ultimatum to make them behave in a certain way. However, manipulation is more devious, influencing employee behaviour through withholding information.

**Marking guide:**
- 2 marks for similarities between manipulation and threat
- 2 marks for differences between manipulation and threat

## Question 3

Artificial intelligence (AI) can improve the efficiency and effectiveness of operations in a variety of ways.

Amazon is an innovative, large-scale organisation that has integrated AI into many of its business systems to be more efficient and effective.

Amazon is increasing efficiency by using facial recognition in Amazon Go stores to remove the need for a checkout, as well as smart robots, like chat bots, to respond to customer queries and in warehouses to automate picking and packaging. To improve productivity, robots can operate around the clock without breaks and, although initially very expensive to design and purchase, do not have the ongoing labour costs associated with human resources, resulting in cost efficiencies.

To more effectively achieve business objectives, at Amazon AI is learning customer needs via search types and now makes product recommendations that result in around 35% of total sales. Amazon's virtual assistant, Alexa, caters to customer needs by learning individual preferences and then recommending products. Alexa also helps Amazon to more effectively meet the business objective of fulfilling a market need, as it adds to the customer experience of convenience through user-friendly applications to support customers integrating technology into their newly 'smart' homes.

**Marking guide (global marking):**
- 1–2 marks for a limited description of how artificial intelligence improves efficiency and/or effectiveness, with no clear links to a relevant case study
- 3–4 marks for some detail about the relationship between the implementation of artificial intelligence and improvements in efficiency and effectiveness, with some links to a relevant case study
- 5–6 marks for comprehensive detail about the relationship between the implementation of artificial intelligence and improvements in efficiency and effectiveness, with multiple links to a relevant case study

## Question 4

a   A human resource manager deals with employees, including recruitment, selection, workplace agreements, worker motivation, training, dispute resolution, succession planning and termination. Labour is a key input in business operations, because without employees, the core work would not get done.

Chow Chow operates across seven locations, requiring a human resource manager to manage the workforce across multiple sites and geographic areas. With eight more restaurants planned, the human resource manager at Chow Chow will need to design job descriptions, advertise positions and shortlist and interview candidates. They would then ensure effective induction and training for the new employees.

**Marking guide:**
- 2 marks for detailing aspects of the human resource manager role
- 1 mark for linking closely to Chow Chow

b   The Four Drive Theory says that every employee has instinctual needs that drive their behaviour, so if a manager can determine which to emphasise for each employee, they can motivate the worker to turn up and be productive.

The human resource manager at Chow Chow can motivate employees who are driven to acquire by strategies such as providing incentives and recognition. The manager could also run promotions for existing employees to take on higher levels of responsibility at the new restaurants, because they have historical business knowledge and this will encourage them to take fewer days off.

To satisfy the drive to bond, teamwork can be emphasised, or the manager can provide opportunities to collaborate, maintain work rituals and celebrations, or share best practice, such as encouraging existing teams to share practices with workers at the eight new locations. Employees with strong work relationships are less likely to be absent.

If workers are interested in learning, the manager could organise new skills training, build challenges into their work or provide opportunities for new roles or responsibilities, helping employees to feel both stimulated and valued, and thus less likely to be absent.

The last drive is to defend. The human resources managers can satisfy this drive (and ensure employees can be relied on to turn up to work) through strategies such as providing a safe, supportive and non-threatening work environment, as well as transparency and fairness in decision-making.

> **Marking guide:**
> - 3 marks for applying the Four Drive Theory to Chow Chow
> - 1 mark for linking closely to Chow Chow

c   Career advancement refers to providing opportunities for employees to take on new positions, often with higher levels of responsibility.

   During expansion to the eight new locations, employees can be motivated in the short term to make changes or move locations, while still achieving business objectives, through allocating workers new roles with higher pay and ways to learn new skills, or providing more job security, such as through negotiating better work conditions or longer work contracts.

   Long-term motivation at Chow Chow could be encouraged by promoting existing workers and giving them responsibility for new recruits. The higher status, increased influence and improved self-esteem would likely lead to better staff retention in the long term.

> **Marking guide:**
> - 2 marks for a brief explanation of how career advancement can improve short-term motivation at Chow Chow
> - 2 marks for a brief explanation of how career advancement can improve long-term motivation at Chow Chow

# SECTION B – Case study

## Question 1

A relevant business objective for Radlee Pty Ltd would be to fulfil a market need. This refers to Radlee Pty Ltd catering to customer wants and needs that are not currently being serviced by businesses in the industry. For example, customers may be seeking lightweight bikes for easy transport to mountain bike trails and Radlee Pty Ltd is therefore using carbon fibre for construction.

> **Marking guide:**
> - 1 mark for a brief explanation of the selected business objective
> - 1 mark for an appropriate example linked to Radlee Pty Ltd

## Question 2

A materials management strategy to improve the efficiency of Radlee Pty Ltd operations would be materials requirement planning (MRP). MRP refers to careful planning of all resources needed to produce the product, where to get them from and when. In this case, that would include the component parts as delivered including carbon fibre frames, tyres, seats and handlebars from China, as well as all other materials required to make the product, such as brakes, cables, branding stickers and paint. MRP increases efficiency as it reduces waste from the system that might be caused by things such as overordering, or delays while waiting for parts not ordered in time. Radlee Pty Ltd currently has levels of waste of 4%, but has been at 3% in the past, so is now seeking sustainable reduction strategies.

> **Marking guide:**
> - 1 mark for suggesting an appropriate materials management strategy
> - 2 marks for providing reason(s) linked to Radlee Pty Ltd

## Question 3

With workplace accidents up from 8 to 13 in the latest recording period, one driving force to reduce this increase at Radlee Pty Ltd could be employees. Employees want safe workplaces and so may be willing to make changes in the way they behave or complete their work to reduce the likelihood of workplace accidents. The legal requirement is that workers leave the workplace in the same state in which they arrived, and employees would be very interested in protecting themselves and their colleagues from harm and could therefore drive a change in practices.

A restraining force for change could be time. Employees may be more than willing to make changes; however, set production targets may require them to work at a speed that does not allow for more careful safety practices. Time is a restraining force that must be considered, with more time allocated to work safer, in order to avoid workplace accidents.

**Marking guide:**
- 2 marks for providing detail about a relevant driving force
- 2 marks for providing detail about a relevant restraining force

## Question 4

Radlee Pty Ltd could use various management strategies to seek new business opportunities, including redeployment of resources and innovation.

Redeployment of resources involves reallocating human or capital resources to new business areas in order to improve business efficiency. For example, employees already in the labour force could be taken off their current duties and redeployed to focus on new areas such as online sales and marketing. This move would allow workers to redirect their efforts in order to seek new business opportunities through attracting more mountain bike customers. Human resources may also be redeployed to assist others in times of urgency, such as before Christmas (e.g. completing large orders in a shorter timeframe), allowing Radlee Pty Ltd to seek out potential US-based clients, who could be bigger clients than Radlee Pty Ltd has been able to service during peak periods in the past.

Radlee Pty Ltd is already using robotic and automated production line technology. However, further innovative improvements to operation processes, such as new or improved technology designs, may allow Radlee Pty Ltd to seek business opportunities through producing new product lines or running aligned complementary businesses through patenting its innovative equipment.

**Marking guide (global marking):**
- 1–2 marks for a limited description of how one or more strategies can be used by Radlee Pty Ltd to seek new business opportunities
- 3–4 marks for some detail about how two strategies can be used by Radlee Pty Ltd to seek new business opportunities
- 5–6 marks for comprehensive detail about how two strategies can be used by Radlee Pty Ltd to seek new business opportunities

## Question 5

Business objectives are the goals, linked to business performance, that Radlee Pty Ltd aims to achieve, such as increasing sales or reducing waste. These targets cannot be met, however, without the support of stakeholders. As parties with a vested interest in Radlee Pty Ltd, different stakeholders have varied and sometimes opposing perspectives. While it is difficult to keep all stakeholders satisfied, Radlee Pty Ltd must attempt to meet the needs of stakeholders to achieve business success.

Stakeholder groups of Radlee Pty Ltd include owners, managers, employees, customers, suppliers and the general community. Owners are interested in achieving business objectives such as increased sales by increasing exports, operations efficiencies (such as the use of robotics) and business sustainability. However, these cannot be achieved without meeting other stakeholder needs. Employees are interested in things like safe and stable work, fair wages and sufficient training to give them confidence to perform their duties. Customers may be focused on product price or quality, reputation or corporate social responsibility considerations. Suppliers want to be paid for their work on time and to develop relationships with Radlee Pty Ltd that ensure ongoing work. The general community may be interested in environmental considerations of Radlee Pty Ltd's operations, or business impacts such as levels of local employment.

Stakeholder interests may conflict, which could be a challenge for Radlee Pty Ltd to manage and satisfy. Managers may be working towards increasing exports by 25% but this may be in direct conflict with employee interests like wanting job security, as this operational change may lead to outsourcing of the sales function to a team in the US. Owners may have different expectations of suppliers as they alter the strategies used to manage materials (e.g. implementing Just in Time), while suppliers may have long lead times and may not be able to cater to changing needs. Owners may also delay paying suppliers to have full use of financial resources, while suppliers may be expecting payment for their service to use the funds for their own businesses. Customers want affordable prices, but affordability is different for every individual circumstance, so it can be difficult for managers to set prices that achieve increases in sales while still remaining attractive to a wide variety of customers. Further, international customers may be adversely affected by an increase in prices through high export costs. Owners may be interested solely in a return on their investment, in the form of dividends when Radlee Pty Ltd makes a profit, while customers may be focused on product quality that cannot be achieved by using the kinds of less-expensive inputs that would cut resource costs to increase profits.

Business change involves transformation that can impact stakeholders and so, if Radlee Pty Ltd is to pursue objectives successfully during periods of change, it is particularly important to align goals with stakeholder needs. Employees want stable work and this can feel threatened when undergoing change, such as implementing new strategies to reduce waste or manage materials. Therefore, to retain workers, Radlee Pty Ltd must reassure employees of their ongoing place in the organisation through providing extended work agreements, training or career advancement. Customers may be uncomfortable with changes to products or production methods and may switch to a more familiar or stable competitor. Radlee Pty Ltd needs to find out customer perspectives to be able to cater for them during change. For example, if customers are interested in innovation, this can be a key message to communicate through marketing, when a new or improved product is released. While it can be difficult to always meet the needs of all stakeholders while pursuing business objectives, organisations must work towards aligning with different stakeholder goals to achieve business success and most particularly during unsettling times of business change.

**Marking guide (global marking):**
- 1–3 marks for a limited description of the relationship between stakeholders and business objectives of Radlee Pty Ltd; some dot points are addressed briefly or not addressed
- 4–7 marks for detailed consideration of the relationship between stakeholders and business objectives of Radlee Pty Ltd; all dot points are addressed with some detail or some dot points are addressed with detail
- 8–10 marks for sophisticated consideration of the relationship between stakeholders and business objectives of Radlee Pty Ltd; all dot points are addressed in a thorough manner

## Question 6

Porter's differentiation approach refers to businesses standing out from their competitors by offering something different that is not otherwise available. This may be in relation to the quality of the product or service, some unique position, like being local to customers and so able to deliver quickly, or using only local labour or materials in production.

The advantages of differentiating a business include making products more attractive than those of competitors, being able to charge a premium price, as this product is difficult to source otherwise, and promoting higher customer loyalty.

Disadvantages of differentiating a business include that it can be costly to change aspects of production or extend product lines, and that making changes is time-consuming for all the departments involved. Also, changes may not keep up with consumer tastes or may be copied by rivals.

Radlee Pty Ltd has set the target of increasing exports to 25% of sales by 2030. The differentiation approach could be used to achieve this goal by advertising Radlee Pty Ltd's unique proposition to potential customers overseas. Promotions might be in relation to corporate social responsibility considerations, the lightweight nature of the product or the fact that Radlee Pty Ltd holds the patent for its suspension system and so is an expert in manufacturing bikes with this innovation, as well as the only business legally allowed to do so. Despite taking time and resources, if Radlee Pty Ltd can differentiate before its competitors copy its innovations, this strategy will allow it to charge a premium price for its bikes, as well as attract international customers, achieving the set objective to increase exports.

**Marking guide:**
- 3 marks for advantages of differentiation approach with links to Radlee Pty Ltd
- 3 marks for disadvantages of differentiation approach with links to Radlee Pty Ltd

### Question 7

Like all businesses, Radlee Pty Ltd needs to consider corporate social responsibility (CSR), because if its stakeholders' wants and values are not aligned to those of the business, employees may leave for other employment, and customers may switch to competitors, boycott products or damage Radlee Pty Ltd's business reputation through actions like negative online reviews. Special-interest groups or the general community may even take legal action against the business. So for future business viability, and especially stakeholder acceptance during change, it is very important to consider CSR when making business decisions.

During changes to meet the new business goals, it is important for Radlee Pty Ltd to consider CSR; for example, workplace safety, particularly in light of increasing workplace accident figures. Using new technologies or new work processes may require dedicated training and time for employees to be safer at work. Radlee Pty Ltd must implement safe practices above and beyond legal requirements, in order to show stakeholders it is committed to keeping its workforce safe.

When integrating new technologies, when Radlee Pty Ltd may be able to cut waste or improve the management of materials, it is important to consider whether a change is morally or ethically supported, such as downsizing the workforce due to newly modified or automated production processes. To maintain stakeholder support, Radlee Pty Ltd will need to weigh up stakeholder interests against business interests and make decisions with CSR in mind.

**Marking guide:**
- 2 marks for explaining the importance of considering corporate social responsibility
- 2 marks for closely linking to business change at Radlee Pty Ltd

# PRACTICE EXAM 2

## SECTION A

### Question 1

a  Human resource management refers to establishing, developing, maintaining and terminating the formal work relationship between employers and employees. Having recently hired 30 new staff, recruitment and selection have already occurred, so a human resource manager at AssetArt would focus on inducting new employees into business practices and corporate culture, training employees, motivating employees to be productive and terminating the work relationship if things don't work out as planned.

**Marking guide:**
- 1 mark for providing characteristic(s) of human resource management
- 1 mark for added detail or link(s) to AssetArt Pty Ltd

**b** Human resources are the labour workforce required by a business to get the core work done. The objective 'to fulfil a market need' refers to the business determining a gap in the market, whereby there are customer wants that are not being satisfied, and the organisation then works to service that need. In relation to AssetArt, the current market need is to own and trade NFT art and, with highly skilled, creative employees trained to use state-of-the-art technology, this niche business is expanding quickly as its specialist staff can provide the products that are in demand. Human resources are essential to achieving business objectives: without employees, a business would not be able to meet targets or goals, as there would be no one to do the actual work.

> **Marking guide:**
> - 1 mark for briefly describing the characteristics of the objective 'to fulfil a market need'
> - 1 mark for demonstrating the relationship between human resources and achieving business objectives
> - 1 mark for close link(s) to AssetArt

**c** The management skill of delegation involves a manager handing down tasks to employees while still retaining the overall responsibility for that job. To effectively delegate, managers must ensure workers have the right skills to complete tasks to the expected quality. Birrani and Max have hired senior artists and graphic designers, meaning these workers already have experience and related skillsets. The partners can trust these expert employees and should delegate by handing over more complex tasks and duties to be completed autonomously. The advantages of delegating include workers feeling empowered and valued; in this case it might make senior employees more connected and satisfied with their jobs. Handing down decision-making authority may also better utilise the expertise they have hired, resulting in more innovative business decisions. Disadvantages of delegation include Birrani and Max losing some control over decision-making and meeting deadlines, and also that employees may misuse power by working towards their personal goals, rather than those of AssetArt, such as spending work time and resources looking for new jobs.

> **Marking guide:**
> - 2 marks for advantages of delegation linked to AssetArt
> - 2 marks for disadvantages of delegation linked to AssetArt

**d** Awards and agreements are methods of making legally binding arrangements that set out conditions guiding the work relationship between employer and employee.

One difference between an award and an agreement is that an award includes the minimum wages and conditions allowed by the Fair Work Commission (FWC) and as set out in the National Employment Standards, whereas an agreement can offer other conditions, as long as they make the worker better off overall than they would have been by following the award.

A second difference is that standardised industry awards are made by the FWC, but agreements are approved by the FWC, meaning that they can be tailored towards individual business and employee objectives.

I fully agree with the human resource manager's recommendation to move to an agreement, as offering wages and conditions higher than the award would allow AssetArt to attract talented people and retain staff for longer in this high-growth and competitive industry of trading in NFTs. A workplace agreement would also allow AssetArt to offer more incentives to motivate employees, and provide enhanced flexibility, such as working from home, flex-time, parental arrangements and whatever else suits its creative labour force. Therefore, Birrani and Max should take the human resource manager's advice and move to an agreement.

> **Marking guide (global marking):**
> - 1–2 marks for limited description of the differences between an award and an agreement with brief, irrelevant or no analysis
> - 3–4 marks for description of the differences between an award and an agreement with adequate analysis
> - 5–6 marks for extensive description of the differences between an award and an agreement, with detailed analysis supporting an argument for or against an agreement at AssetArt

## Question 2

To stay successful in the dynamic business environment, Australia Post has had to make operational and human resource management changes to manage a steady decline in letters, alongside a rapid increase in e-commerce parcels. To assist with planning to increase efficiency and capacity in dealing with parcels, management may have applied Lewin's Force Field Analysis theory.

Driving forces would need to be identified, such as technological advances and internet availability, as well as customers changing shopping habits facilitating increased online shopping from home, thus causing increased volume of parcels coming through distribution centres. Another driving force could be societal attitudes, in that Australians are now more trusting of e-commerce and so are more likely to order and send product parcels as both consumers and businesses.

Restraining forces against Australia Post making changes may be its employees, who may be use to their work environment and practices and may not want to train or change how they spend their work day. Cost may also be a restraining factor, as new machines that can handle the larger parcels would need to be designed, manufactured, installed and maintained, with employees trained in their use.

Managers would need to assign a weighting to each of these driving and restraining forces to decide which can be emphasised and which must be minimised to encourage a smooth change transition. For example, customer wants and needs could be considered the most important aspect to address through a marketing campaign, to show customers their changing e-commerce needs are supported and encourage ongoing customer loyalty. Employee resistance may be determined as the most important restraining factor to address; without workers on board, productivity drops as the core business does not get done, due to lack of confidence with new processes, passive resistance or staff absenteeism.

Australia Post managers would then need to rank these forces to prioritise according to specified criteria, perhaps based on immediate need, cost, practicality or ease of shifting a restraining factor to a driving factor. Decisions could then be made about change implementation plans to select the best course of action as Australia Post works towards the most efficient and effective transition possible.

**Marking guide (global marking):**
- 1–2 marks for limited description of Lewin's Force Field Analysis with little or no reference to a case study
- 3–4 marks for description of Lewin's Force Field Analysis with some reference to a case study
- 5 marks for detailed description of the principles of Lewin's Force Field Analysis with close reference to a case study

## Question 3

a Official corporate culture refers to the publicised values and expectations of a business. It is part of building business reputation and can be found documented in policies and on public-facing communication channels like websites.

Real corporate culture is how employees actually behave in their day-to-day work. This may or may not follow the official culture expectations for behaviour and language. For example, a business may advertise how environmentally friendly its products are, but in practice, employees may take process shortcuts that create more waste during production, or fail to dispose of operations waste in a sustainable way. The difference between the two terms is that official corporate culture is what the business wants people to think about it, but real culture is what the business and its employees actually say and do when out of the public eye.

**Marking guide:**
- 1 mark for providing characteristic(s) of official corporate culture
- 1 mark for providing characteristic(s) of real corporate culture
- 1 mark for demonstrating the difference between the terms

**b** Two strategies to develop corporate culture when introducing robotics are clear communication and linking increased productivity to rewards.

Clear, well-targeted and regular communications between managers and staff instils a sense of trust because the reasons behind a change can be given, as well as potential impacts on employees and supports that have been put in place to assist them to manage the change. Clear communication encourages an open-dialogue corporate culture and helps employees to be more confident in their new work practices. This particular situation might lead to workforce downsizing, because production processes are being automated; however, clear communication can help to alleviate worry or distress among the workers that remain, thus maintaining a positive corporate culture.

Linking rewards or incentives to increased productivity can assist in the development of a positive corporate culture, with employees willing to make changes, such as new ways of working with and alongside robotics. Employees may be offered monetary bonuses for meeting new targets or perks for completing robotics training, such as retail gift cards or corporate merchandise. Rewards help employees to regard the change as a win for them and so develop a positive attitude to act as a driving force, rather than resisting the change in work requirements or practices. Rewarding employees helps to build a strong and positive corporate culture, whereby most employees see the change as favourable and so continue to work towards business objectives.

**Marking guide (global marking):**
- 1–2 marks for giving one or two strategies for developing corporate culture when introducing robotics, with little or no justification
- 3–4 marks for providing one or two relevant strategies for developing corporate culture when introducing robotics, with some justification(s)
- 5–6 marks for providing two relevant strategies for developing corporate culture when introducing robotics, with well-linked justifications

## Question 4

This statement is problematic. When responding to competition, businesses can improve their products as well as simultaneously bring out the best in their employees.

Competition brings out the best in people through improving the corporate culture so it strives for excellence, while working towards achieving business objectives, in a more team-spirited and focused way. Pursuing a differentiation strategy to become more competitive can result in innovation that improves operations for workers, making their jobs easier, safer and more interesting to perform.

To gain a competitive advantage, businesses may implement motivation strategies that benefit employees and positively impact how satisfied they are with their work. Management styles may shift to more consultative or participative approaches to more fully engage employees in change through empowerment. Valuing individual opinion and effort may drive workers to take ownership to continuously improve business systems, causing them to develop stronger connections to their work and loyalty to their employer, while increasing competitiveness.

Competitive business behaviour can also negatively impact workers in that the cost cutting associated with pursuing a lower-cost strategy can result in employees taking shortcuts in production processes that may lead to workplace accidents. Cost cuts may also come from using lower-quality inputs, resulting in inferior final products that employees must then falsely market to convince others to purchase. Workers may feel a disconnection between their own values and the products they are making or selling.

Downsizing may be the strategy chosen to increase competitiveness, so employees may feel pitted against one another to keep the remaining jobs, or distressed as their colleagues are made redundant, so they worry about both their friends and their own positions. Changes such as introducing technology or outsourcing to improve products may also lead to job losses, causing similar types of employee anxiety or resistance, possible employee conflict and workplace disputes.

Although some strategies to achieve business competitiveness can result in negative impacts on employees, bringing out resistant or unwanted work behaviours, when change is managed well, willing employees can be the greatest asset for a business as they work as a team to gain a competitive advantage, resulting in business sustainability that benefits all. Therefore, the statement is not universally correct.

**Marking guide (global marking):**
- 1–3 marks for limited discussion of the strength(s) and weakness(es) of business competition in relation to human resources
- 4–7 marks for appropriate discussion of the strengths and weaknesses of business competition in relation to human resources, with a brief conclusion, possibly not related to the points raised
- 8–10 marks for extensive discussion of the strengths and weaknesses of business competition in relation to human resources, with a conclusion related to the points raised

## Question 5

**a**  Because Topperz is an online business, one key performance indicator Kate could use to analyse performance is the number of website hits. Website hits indicate how many times Topperz's pages have been clicked on. This indicates the rate of increase or decrease in interested parties, but not necessarily whether they are potential customers, existing customers clicking multiple times or even competitors doing research. Kate could analyse timing of website hits to determine peak periods, in order to better plan for responsive work in times of high demand.

**Marking guide:**
- 1 mark for briefly explaining the selected key performance indicator
- 1 mark for extra detail including linking with Topperz

**b**  Lean production techniques may help Kate respond to key performance indicators. Kate feels like she wastes a lot of time and resources, and lean strategies are focused on reducing waste.

Kate may employ a pull system whereby she does not produce items until they are ordered by a customer. This technique alleviates the issue of wasting input and storage resources on unsold mass, or estimated production, focusing more on effectively meeting actual customer demand.

Another lean production technique is takt. Takt scheduling involves pacing work to a consistent rhythm and to match customer demand. Kate would first need to determine how long it takes to produce a cake topper, then set this as a standard work time for all production. This would ensure that time is not wasted by uneven allocation and thus should result in Kate being able to meet demand more efficiently, increasing overall productivity and related net profit.

**Marking guide:**
- 2 marks for identifying and describing a relevant lean production technique and demonstrating how the technique will impact business performance at Topperz (× 2)

**c**  Kate might expand her product range at Topperz through standardising designs and making the most of overseas production opportunities. Customised products like balloons, bunting and invitations can be sourced from overseas to remove the need to invest in new equipment and to take advantage of lower manufacturing and labour costs. Buying products with the same design in bulk would also lower the cost per unit, although may result in unsold items. Kate can then sell these globally sourced inputs with her corporate branding and for a profit.

**Marking guide:**
- 1 mark for demonstrating an understanding of the general business opportunities of global sourcing
- 1 mark for link(s) to Topperz

**d**  A corporate social responsibility consideration that may influence Kate's decision to expand her product range through global sourcing of inputs might be environmental sustainability. The overseas manufacturer might not be legally required to adhere to strict environmental controls, may create high levels of pollution, or deplete or damage natural resources. Another key environmental consideration is the transport required to secure globally sourced products. Fossil fuel use, pollution of air and oceans and carbon emissions are all possible impacts that may influence Kate's decision-making. Because suppliers are based internationally, Kate may have little oversight of production methods and environmental impacts. Clients may have high expectations about environmental sustainability that Topperz needs to meet to retain their custom.

**Marking guide:**
- 1 mark for suggesting a relevant corporate social responsibility consideration
- 2 marks for showing the cause-and-effect relationship between Topperz using overseas suppliers and the stated corporate social responsibility consideration

## SECTION B – Case study

### Question 1

Social enterprises have the overall aim of fulfilling a social need, such as Comfy Community providing housing for women and families experiencing homelessness or financial difficulties. While operating like commercial businesses, profits do not go to owners, but instead are reinvested into the enterprise. Comfy Community is setting up several business types, like the childcare centre and the bakery, in order to sell to the public and use profits to maintain the community ventures and expand business ventures.

**Marking guide:**
- 1 mark for providing characteristic(s) of a social enterprise
- 1 mark for link(s) to Comfy Community

### Question 2

The community centre is a service provider, offering digital literacy and woodworking classes, financial support services and a wellness gym, whereas the Comfy Bakehouse manufactures products, in particular the popular apple goodies made from orchard fruit.

Both business ventures have the purpose of producing something that meets the needs of customers and is to be sold for a profit. Another similarity is that the community centre and the Comfy Bakehouse can take a quality management approach to use strategies like quality assurance to continuously improve the efficiency and effectiveness of their operations through ensuring high-quality inputs.

Differences between the two types of business include that the Bakehouse's tangible products can be touched and stored, that they may be manufactured in a standardised way without much customer input and that consumption of the apple goodies is separate, and possibly offsite. The community centre classes and services are intangible, in that they cannot be touched physically and only a record of providing the service may be stored. Services, such as gym or financial, may be tailored for the client, and these services are consumed at the time of service, onsite at the community centre.

**Marking guide:**
- 2 marks for demonstrating similarities between the types of business at Comfy Community
- 2 marks for demonstrating differences between the types of business at Comfy Community

### Question 3

One driving force that has positively influenced change at Comfy Community is societal attitudes. Society has become more aware and supportive of older women suffering financial hardship due to divorce, job loss, illness recovery or homelessness. Rock and Zan point out that they could not have built their community without generous donations of time, money and resources from local businesses, the local community and their neighbours. Local government must also have been in favour of this social enterprise development, as it approved planning permissions.

One restraining force that has negatively influenced change at Comfy Community is financial considerations. Although Zan and Rock may have funded the first two tiny houses, paying for 56 more required external funding sources like donations, crowdfunding and government grants. A lack of financial resources may have held them back initially and makes it difficult to sustain the infrastructure needed to service the 120 residents. Consequently, entrepreneurial ventures have been set up to financially sustain the community in the long term. However, these will take some time to cover establishment costs, restraining funding of further change until the businesses start making profits.

**Marking guide:**
- 2 marks for characteristics of a relevant driving force at Comfy Community
- 2 marks for characteristics of a relevant restraining force at Comfy Community

## Question 4

Senge's Learning Organisation refers to a business that aims for continuous positive transformation through facilitating employee learning. The five disciplines or principles are developing a shared vision, systems thinking, mental models, team learning and personal mastery.

Although Rock and Zan have their own personal goals for Comfy Community, to create a positive culture for change they need to involve others in creating a shared vision. This involvement ensures that employees feel valued and part of the organisation, making them more motivated to work towards an agreed vision that fosters genuine commitment, as well as encouraging risk-taking and innovation.

Systems thinking reflects that every action and consequence links to another; all employees are responsible for change and customer feedback is a key driver. The success of the entrepreneurial ventures at Comfy Community may be enhanced, or even rely on, all employees listening to customer wants, and then taking action to service them; for example, about which types of classes are needed at the community centre or the hours clients need the childcare centre services. This is a big business now and requires high-level systems oversight to make positive changes.

Mental models refer to ingrained assumptions such as employee understanding of the reasons Comfy Community exists. Shared underlying values, such as honesty and leadership through service, build a strong corporate culture that is focused on business objectives. Flexibility is also important, as the workforce also needs to be able to shift mental models when a business changes, such as by opening new business ventures or increasing the number of tiny houses on site.

Team learning brings together the shared vision and personal mastery, whereby workers have a clear vision of goals and their individual capacity to achieve objectives. The Comfy Community as a whole needs to be focused on achieving team goals by harnessing collective skills and talents, with workers regarding their colleagues as fellow team members, rather than as rivals. Team spirit is required to make this venture a success, and employees need to foster a work environment where mistakes are forgiven as learning opportunities. This is particularly important as some workers, like Millie, have previously been out of the workforce for a long time and may need retraining to improve their personal mastery and thus be proficient and feel confident at work. Work confidence through personal mastery will help prepare workers for positive responses during business change.

**Marking guide (global marking):**
- 1–2 marks for outlining some or all of the principles of Senge's Learning Organisation, with limited linking to Comfy Community
- 3–4 marks for applying some or all of the principles of Senge's Learning Organisation to Comfy Community business situation, with limited mention of creating and maintaining a positive culture for change
- 5–6 marks for appropriately applying all of the principles of Senge's Learning Organisation to Comfy Community's business situation to create and maintain a positive culture for change

## Question 5

As a quality management strategy, Total Quality Management (TQM) aims for continuous improvement through all employees taking responsibility for positive incremental changes to processes and corporate culture. TQM uses systems thinking by separating operations into inputs, processes and outputs, and then focusing on making positive changes to individual facets, based on customer feedback.

Comfy Community can improve the effectiveness of its operations by implementing TQM business-wide, as the proactive customer focus will improve its commitment to providing products and services that customers want to buy. As sales consequently increase, profits will be earned, allowing Comfy Community to support the wider venture in areas such as building infrastructure, like pathways between the 58 tiny houses. TQM requires Comfy Community to clearly design and articulate its vision, making it part of its corporate culture as to how things are done in its community. This increases worker empowerment and commitment to achieving the goals by encouraging shared responsibility for effectively achieving business outcomes.

However, implementing TQM can be costly and time consuming, as it requires devoted and well-trained human resources that would otherwise be employed in profit-making activities. This might hinder achievement of some business objectives. Gaining oversight would also be difficult, considering the number of varied elements and diversity of business offerings that make up the community. Managing this complexity would redeploy management away from the core business of building and sustaining the community.

**Marking guide:**
- 2 marks for the advantages of implementing the TQM strategy at Comfy Community
- 2 marks for the disadvantages of implementing the TQM strategy at Comfy Community

## Question 6

Rock and Zan are being proactive: they are planning ahead for a smooth change transition rather than using a reactive approach, whereby they would instead respond to something that has already happened.

Forecasting growing future demand from women in financial distress, Rock and Zan sought funding from various sources such as banks, crowdfunding sources and donors. This proactive securing of financial resources has continued over the life of the business as it has expanded, with the owners setting up entrepreneurial ventures to fund future community needs.

Rock and Zan have worked to anticipate and meet the needs of the local community through various targeted facilities and business offerings. Resident needs are catered for through training classes, financial services and wellness facilities at the community centre. Rock and Zan have planned to service the needs of neighbours and the local community by opening a childcare centre, general store and the new bakehouse, simultaneously raising profit to improve the community for a rapidly increasing number 'of residents.

Rock and Zan have made the most of the business opportunities that have arisen, such as noting apple product sales success at markets, then developing a more commercial bakery. They are investing in training and opportunities for residents to build leadership capacity that then allows them to retain talent through career progression within their own business. Woodworking classes may also help in the physical building of their expanding community. All these actions demonstrate Rock and Zan's proactive approach to change management at Comfy Community.

**Marking guide (global marking):**
- 1–2 marks for brief demonstration of whether Rock and Zan are taking a proactive or reactive response to change, with few or no case study examples
- 3–4 marks for demonstration of whether Rock and Zan are taking a proactive or reactive response to change, linked to some case study examples
- 5 marks for detailed demonstration of whether Rock and Zan are taking a proactive or reactive response to change, evidenced by linking to relevant case study examples